Helion & Company Limited
Unit 8 Amherst Business Centre
Budbrooke Road
Warwick
CV34 5WE
England
Tel. 01926 499 619
Email: info@helion.co.uk
Website: www.helion.co.uk
Twitter: @helionbooks
Visit our blog https://helionbooks.wordpress.com/

Typeset by Oliver Barstow, Milan, Italy
Cover design by Paul Hewitt, Battlefield Design (www.battlefield-design.co.uk)

ISBN 978-1-804515-75-4

British Library Cataloguing-in-Publication Data
A catalogue record for this book is available from the British Library

Cover artwork:
A pair of *Força Aérea Brasileira* T-6Ds drop napalm bombs and strafe guerrillas in the jungle, while a Cessna L-19 Bird Dog acts forward air controller. (Artwork by Renato Dalmaso)

CONTENTS

Note: In order to simplify the use of this book, all names, locations and geographic designations are as provided in *The Times World Atlas*, or other traditionally accepted major sources of reference, as of the time of described events.

ABBREVIATIONS AND ACRONYMS

AFB	Air Force Base
ALADA	*1ª Asa de Defesa Aérea* (1st Air Defence Wing) (FAB)
ARENA	*Aliança Renovadora Nacional* (National Renewal Alliance)
BIS	*Batalhão de Infantaria de Selva* (Jungle Infantry Battalion) (Brazilian Army)
CECAN	*Centro do Corréio Aéreo Nacional* (National Air Mail Centre) (FAB)
CATRE	*Centro de Aplicações Táticas e Recomplementamento de Equipagens* (Tactical Applications and Equipment Replenishment Centre) (FAB)
CCC	*Comando de Caça aos Comunistas* (Command for Hunting Communists)
CENIMAR	*Centro de Informações da Marinha* (Navy Information Centre)
CFN	*Corpo de Fuzileiros Navais* (Marine Corps) (Brazilian Navy)
CFPM	*Centro de Formação de Pilotos Militares* (Military Pilot Training Centre) (FAB)
CIA	Central Intelligence Agency (US)
CIEH	*Centro de Instrução e Emprego de Helicópteros* (Helicopter Training and Utilisation Centre) (FAB)
CIEX	*Centro de Inteligência do Exército* (Army Intelligence Centre)
CNBB	*Conferência Nacional dos Bispos do Brasil* (National Conference of Bishops of Brazil)
DF	*Distrito Federal* (Federal District)
DOI-CODI	*Destacamento de Operações Internas-Comando Operacional de Defesa Interna* (Detachment of Internal Operations-Operational Command of Internal Defence)
DOPS	*Departamento Estadual de Ordem Política e Social* (State Department of Political and Social Order) (Federal Police)
EB	*Exército Brasileiro* (Brazilian Army)
ECA	*Esquadrão de Comunicações e Alerta* (Communications and Alert Squadron) (FAB)
EDA	*Esquadrão de Demonstração Aérea* (Air Demonstration Squadron) (FAB)
EIA	*Esquadrão de Instrução Aérea* (Air Instruction Squadron) (FAB)
ELO	*Esquadrilha de Ligação e Observação* (Liaison and Observation Squadron) (FAB)
EMBRAER	*Empresa Brasileira de Aeronáutica S.A.* (Brazilian Aeronautics Company, Inc.)
EMRA	*Esquadrão Misto de Reconhecimento e Ataque* (Reconnaissance and Attack Mixed Squadron) (FAB)
ERA	*Esquadrão de Reconhecimento e Ataque* (Reconnaissance and Attack Squadron) (FAB)
ETA	*Esquadrão de Transporte Aéreo* (Air Transport Squadron) (FAB)
FAB	*Força Aérea Brasileira* (Brazilian Air Force)
FOGUERA	*Força de Guerilha do Araguaia* (Araguaia Guerrilla Force)
GAE	*Grupo de Aviação Embarcada* (Embarked Air Group) (FAB)
GAV	*Grupo de Aviação* (Aviation Group) (FAB)
GAvCA	*Grupo de Aviação de Caça* (Air Fighter Group) (FAB)
GDA	*Grupo de Defesa Aérea* (Air Defence Group) (FAB)
GDP	Gross Domestic Product
Gr11	*Grupos dos Onze* (Groups of Eleven)
GTA	Araguaia Working Group
GT	*Grupo de Transporte* (Transport Group) (FAB)
GTE	*Grupo de Transporte Especial* (Special Transport Group) (FAB)
GTT	*Grupo de Transporte de Tropas* (Troop Transport Group) (FAB)
LCU	Landing Craft Utility
LCVP	Landing Craft, Vehicle, Personnel (Higgins Boat)
MAC	Anti-Communist Movement
MB	*Marinha do Brasil* (Brazilian Navy)
MDB	*Movimento Democrático Brasileiro* (Brazilian Democratic Movement)
MR-8	*Movimento Revolucionário 8 de Outubro* (8 October Revolutionary Movement)
MRMN	*Movimento de Resistência Militar Nacionalista* (Nationalist Military Resistance Movement)
MRT	*Movimento Revolucionário Tiradentes* (Tiradentes Revolutionary Movement)
OBAN	*Operação Bandeirantes* (Operation Bandeirantes)
PCB	*Partido Comunista Brasileiro* (Brazilian Communist Party)
PCBR	*Partido Comunista Brasileiro Revolucionário* (Brazilian Revolutionary Communist Party)
PCdoB	*Partido Comunista do Brasil* (Communist Party of Brazil)
PCR	*Partido Comunista Revolucionário* (Revolutionary Communist Party)
PDS	*Partido Democrático Social* (Social Democratic Party)
PF	*Polícia Federal* (Federal Police)
PIC	*Pelotão de Investigações Criminais* (Criminal Investigation Platoon) (Army)
PM	*Polícia Militar* (Military Police)
PMDB	*Partido do Movimento Democrático Brasileiro* (Brazilian Democratic Movement Party)
POLOP	*Organização Revolucionária Marxista Política Operária* (Marxist Revolutionary Workers Political Organisation)
PRT	*Partido Revolucionário dos Trabalhadores* (Workers' Revolutionary Party)
PT	*Partido dos Trabalhadores* (Workers' Party)
PTB	*Partido Trabalhista Brasileiro* (Brazilian Labour Party)

RAN	*Resistência Armada Nacionalista* (Nationalist Armed Resistance)
SNI	*Serviço Nacional de Informações* (National Information Service)
UNE	*União Nacional dos Estudantes* (National Union of Students)
VAR-Palmares	*Vanguarda Armada Revolucionaria-Palmares* (Revolutionary Armed Vanguard-Palmares)
VPR	*Vanguarda Popular Revolucionária* (Popular Revolutionary Vanguard)

ACKNOWLEDGEMENTS

The author wishes to express his deep gratitude to fellow Brazilian historian Hélio Higuchi for his invaluable help in the preparation of this volume, both with data and pictures. Without his help, this book would probably remain incomplete.

INTRODUCTION

The *Guerrilha do Araguaia* (Araguaia Guerrilla) was an armed conflict in Brazil against its military government, active between 1967 and 1974 in the Araguaia River basin, in the states of Maranhão, Pará and Goiás in the heart of the Amazon region, in an area known as the Bico do Papagaio (Parrot Beak). It was founded by militants of the Communist Party of Brazil (*Partido Comunista do Brasil*, PCdoB), the then Maoist counterpart of the Brazilian Communist Party (*Partido Comunista Brasileiro*, PCB), which aimed to establish a rural bastion from which to wage a 'people's war' against the Brazilian military, which had been in power since the 1964 *coup d'état*. Its planned activities were based on the successes of the Communist 26th of July Movement in the Cuban Revolution and the Chinese Communist Party during the Chinese Civil War in 1949.

This volume is divided into three chapters. The first chapter briefly describes the military regimes in Brazil between 1964 and 1985 and is followed by a chapter on the subversive groups – both urban and rural – that appeared in the country in the late 1960s and early 1970s. The third chapter is dedicated to a description of the organisation of the Brazilian armed military and police forces in the 1960s and 1970s. Volume 2 will describe the armed forces' operations against the insurgents in Araguaia in the Amazon region and the actions of the guerrillas, as well as the events following the defeat of the guerrillas and a final evaluation of the situation.

1

THE MILITARY REGIMES IN BRAZIL, 1964–1985

Background

In the 1960 elections in Brazil, Jânio da Silva Quadros of the Christian Democratic Party (*Partido Democrata Cristão*, PDC) was elected President with 48.26 percent of the votes cast, and João Belchior Marques Goulart of the Brazilian Labour Party (*Partido Trabalhista Brasileiro*, PTB) became the Vice President.

President Jânio da Silva Quadros (left) and Vice President João Belchior Marques Goulart (right). (Open Source)

On Friday, 25 August 1961, President Jânio Quadros resigned from his position after only seven months of his government. In theory, his resignation was the first step towards a 'self-coup', as he thought that Congress, the armed forces and even the people in general would not accept the resignation. He would thus return to the presidency in the face of such a massive request and ask Congress for more powers than those established in the 1946 Constitution. Deep down, he wanted not only to be a strong president but a dictator. However, Congress accepted his resignation and he had to leave office permanently. According to the then constitution of Brazil, the Vice President was to assume the presidency. However, Goulart, who at the time was on a trip to Eastern Europe, the Soviet Union and the People's Republic of China as a representative of the Brazilian government, was vetoed by the military cabinet ministers for security reasons, and above all because he was very close to the unions and left-wing politicians, and this was unacceptable to the armed forces. The President of the Chamber of Representatives, Pascoal Ranieri Mazzilli, second in the line of presidential succession, assumed power for 14 days until Goulart managed to take over the government on 2 September, after the approval by Congress of an amendment to the 1946 Constitution,

Pascoal Ranieri Mazzilli, President of the Chamber of Representatives (left), and João Goulart, known as *Jango*, finally assumed the Presidency of Brazil after Quadros' resignation. (Open Source)

President João Goulart (left) and the governor of Rio Grande do Sul, Leonel de Moura Brizola (right). Their smiles would end shortly after. (Open Source)

by which a parliamentary system of government was established to replace the existing presidential one.

After a long period of negotiation, led by Goulart's brother-in-law, Leonel de Moura Brizola, at the time governor of Rio Grande do Sul, the Vice President's supporters and the opposition in Congress reached a political agreement, and by more than 1,500 votes in favour decided to sign a political agreement by which a parliamentary regime was created. Goulart's power was reduced by the terms of this agreement, although he maintained the title of Head of State, while the head of the government would be a prime minister. On Saturday, 2 September 1961, Brazil thus became a parliamentary democracy.

According to the constitutional amendment that created the Brazilian parliamentary system, all acts of the President of the Republic had to be endorsed by the Prime Minister. In the adopted model,

Tancredo de Almeida Neves (left), the first Prime Minister of Brazil between 1961 and 1962, Francisco Brochado da Rocha (centre), the second Prime Minister in 1962, and Hermes Lima (right), third Prime Minister between 1962 and 1963, when the post was abolished. (Open source)

it was up to the President to appoint the Prime Minister and form the Council of Ministers, which would have to be approved by two-thirds of Congress. It was not possible for the President to dissolve Congress. The chosen Prime Minister was Tancredo de Almeida Neves, who assumed power on 7 September 1961, the same day that Goulart took office as President under the new regime. Tancredo Neves was succeeded by Francisco Brochado da Rocha in 1962, and later by Hermes Lima.

Despite having prepared proposals to develop the economy and combat the public deficit and inflation, the parliamentary regime did not allow Goulart to approve such plans, due to the lack of a consistent political coalition. Because of the failure of parliamentarism, he organised a plebiscite in which the population would decide whether the parliamentary regime continued or if the presidential system should be reestablished. In 1963, the majority of the population supported the return of presidentialism and Goulart began to put in place reforms in the economy that would allow a better distribution of income, which were known as the Basic Reforms.

The Basic Reforms prevented agrarian, tax, administrative, banking and educational reform, the nationalisation of foreign companies and the application of the Remittance Control Law to control the sending of interest to the parent companies of foreign companies. In March 1963, for example, the Rural Worker Statute, authored by deputy Fernando Ferrari, was approved in Congress, through which rural workers began to have the same rights as urban workers. The government had support from the unions, the General Confederation of Workers (*Confederação Geral dos Trabalhadores*, CGT), the communists and socialists, but was strongly opposed by businessmen, large rural landowners, the military and sectors of the middle class. In Congress, the President also came up against strong opposition from the National Democratic Union (*União Democrática Nacional*, UDN) and the Social Democratic Party (*Partido Democrático Social*, PDS).

Goulart strove to sustain the non-aligned foreign policy of Jânio Quadros, with emphasis on the pursuit of economic development. Thus, the 'East–West dispute' was replaced by a 'North–South conflict', and he moved away from the Cold War as the driving axis of foreign policy.

The Basic Reforms and independent foreign policy were considered to be socialist by Brazil's military, the political opposition, landowners and businessmen. It should be remembered that Goulart's predecessor, Jânio Quadros, had been pressured to resign for having sought rapprochement with communist countries (especially Cuba and the People's Republic of China) without breaking ties with the United States. As Brazil was fundamental to the political interests of the US government, and foreign policy decisions affected its interests, relations between the two countries worsened. Washington then began to support the opposition to the Brazilian government, even preparing to activate Operation Brother Sam, under which the US Navy and Air Force would help enable a coup.

President Goulart was very popular among common people (left), but not with landowners, businessmen, the upper classes and above all the military (right). (Open Source)

The then Brigadier General Humberto de Alencar Castelo Branco, Brazilian Army Chief of Staff in 1963, a Second World War veteran. (Open source)

In October 1963, a new crisis began after an interview by an American journalist with Governor Carlos Lacerda, in opposition to Goulart, in which he violently attacked the government and the President. The military considered the interview offensive to the armed forces and suggested that Goulart declare a state of siege. The President supported the idea, and sent the proposal to Congress. However, the governing party, the PTB, decided not to support the idea, fearing the suppression of political freedoms. Feeling isolated, the President withdrew the proposal and began to lose political and military control of the situation. Many military graduates who had refused to participate in the conspiracy now began to support their radical comrades. Along with all the threats coming from the right-wing, Goulart also faced the worsening of relations with leftist forces, who declared in mid-October that the President was carrying out a government of exclusive interest to the conservative classes.[1]

The military had already decided that Goulart was leading Brazil toward a socialist state which would liquidate the country's traditional values and institutions, so they started conspiring to overthrow the President. The coordinator of the military conspirators was the Army Chief of Staff, General Humberto de Alencar Castelo Branco. He was a quiet, reserved soldier who, as a young officer, had been in combat in Italy during 1944–1945 with the Brazilian Expeditionary Force as part of the US Fifth Army. The conspirators were strongly anti-communist and all of them were graduates of the *Escola Superior de Guerra* (Higher War School), modelled after the US National War College. According to them, the primary threat was not from an external invasion but internally through leftist labour unions, intellectuals, peasant unions, clerics and university students.

At the beginning of 1964, Brazil's economy was suffering serious problems due to a reduction in investment and the cost of state intervention in the national economy. Inflation rose considerably and the political struggle between Goulart and the right-wing opposition increased. Within the armed forces there were plans to force President Goulart to renounce his reforms and displace his leftist allies from the government administration. Goulart still trusted in the loyalty of a group of officers promoted to high positions during his mandate, and in the possibility that their supporters could put up armed resistance to a military uprising.

On Friday, 13 March 1964, in a large assembly in the public square next to the Central Railway Station in Rio de Janeiro, Goulart signed a decree of expropriation of private oil refineries and authorised the seizing of lands 20km from the edge of roads, railways, navigable rivers and dams. In addition, he asked for a new constitution for the country. Approximately 130,000 people were in attendance to hear his speech.

The decrees of 13 March provoked a reaction from conservatives, who organised the so-called Family March with God for Freedom. The first of these occurred in São Paulo on 19 March, St Joseph's Day, the Catholic Church's patron of the family and workers. The main organiser of the march was the deputy Antônio Sílvio da Cunha Bueno, supported by Governor Adhemar de Barros, an opponent of Goulart. The march ended outside the city's cathedral, with a mass 'for the salvation of democracy'.[2]

Two events in March 1964, days before the *coup d'état*: the Family March with God for Freedom (left) and the Sailors' Assembly (right), both protesting against Goulart's government. (Open source)

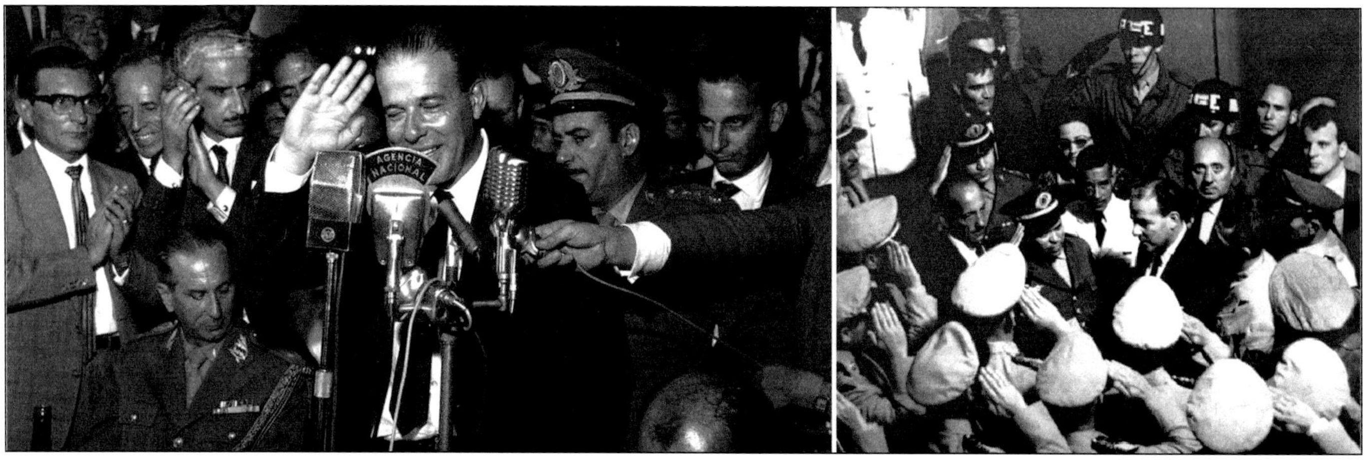

The last speech of President Goulart at the Automobile Club of Rio de Janeiro on 30 March 1964. The *coup d'état* began the next day. (*O Globo*).

An assembly of sailors in Rio de Janeiro on Wednesday, 25 March 1964, demanding an increase in salaries, generated an almost total break by Goulart with the military hierarchy. Some 2,000 sailors, commanded by José Anselmo dos Santos, who became known as *Corporal Anselmo*, were present, and with them was Leonel Brizola. The Minister of the Navy, Sílvio Mota, ordered the imprisonment of the sailors who took part in the assembly and sent the *Fuzileiros Navais* (the Navy's Marine Corps) to carry out the arrests of the mutineers. However, the *Fuzileiros* joined the rebels, with the support of their commander, Admiral Cândido Aragão. On Thursday, 26 March, an agreement was reached with the mutineers for them to surrender, and they were immediately prosecuted for insubordination, but the President granted them an amnesty shortly after.

As Goulart made a definite turn to the political Left, he did not find it united. The conspirators then moved quickly. With Castelo Branco achieving the support of the vast majority of the armed forces, a military coup was underway. On Monday, 30 March, President Goulart made an impromptu speech at the Automobile Club of Rio de Janeiro before a troop of sergeants and demanded military support for his reforms. This was the signal to the coup plotters to act.

The 1964 Military Coup

On the night of Tuesday, 31 March 1964, General Olímpio Mourão Filho, head of the Minas Geráis garrison, began the revolt, advancing with his troops towards Rio de Janeiro, where President Goulart then was. On the same day, the US Embassy in Brazil began Operation Brother Sam, the objective of which was to ensure the success of the coup. Immediately, the coup movement gained followers within the armed forces. During the afternoon, the Chief of Staff of the Army (based in Rio de Janeiro), General Castelo Branco, tried in vain to stop the plotters in their march, alleging that the support of São Paulo's troops was not assured. The head of the Second Army (based in São Paulo), General Amaury Kruel, telephoned Goulart on the night of 31 March to ask him to resign or dismiss his leftist advisors, but the President refused his request, criticising the general for asking him to make such a humiliating decision. Goulart even declared: 'General, you must cling to your convictions. Put your troops on the street and publicly betray me.'[3] After General Kruel's failed attempt to get Goulart to stand down, the São Paulo troops joined the mutiny.

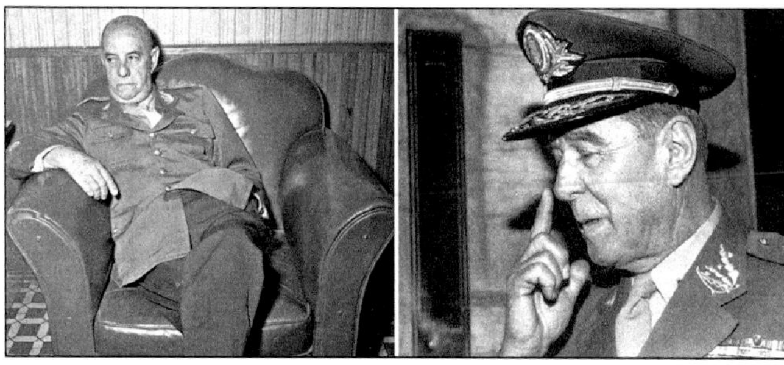

Two key senior officers in the success of the 1964 coup: Army General Olímpio Mourão Filho (left) and Major General Amaury Kruel (right). (Open source)

Goulart dismissed the first news of the revolt and planned to resist, relying on the Army's divisions garrisoned in southern Brazil (his

Brazilian Army M41 Walker Bulldog tanks on the streets of Rio de Janeiro (left) and near the Goulart Presidential Residence (right) on 31 March 1964. (*Exército Brasileiro*).

Troops, tanks and armoured vehicles were everywhere during the 1964 coup. On the left, a military column led by an M3A1 Stuart light tank on a street in São Paulo. On the right, another military column on a road with several M8 Greyhound armoured vehicles, jeeps, Stuart tanks and trucks. (João Marques; *Exército Brasileiro*)

native region) that he believed were loyal to him, counting on troops from Paraíba and Rio Grande do Sul. However, none of the senior officers could be contacted; the plotters had chosen a date when the generals who were possibly still loyal to Goulart were on vacation, on rest, or away from their garrisons for some reason.

With no ability to resist, João Goulart left Rio de Janeiro and travelled to Brasília at noon on Wednesday, 1 April, but there he found that Congress, dominated by the right-wing opposition, planned to declare its vacancy, and refused to support him against the coup plotters. That same afternoon, Goulart flew to Porto Alegre on an Air Force (*Força Aérea Brasileira*, FAB) plane planning to resist the rebellion from there and waiting for the First Army to be deployed (stationed on the outskirts of Rio de Janeiro). Meanwhile, Leonel Brizola demanded armed resistance to the coup, but such calls came to naught. That same afternoon, General Armando de Moraes Âncora, head of the First Army, tried to oppose the revolt but, faced with the risk of unleashing conflict between Brazilian soldiers (a situation that all military leaders wanted to prevent), he gave up his efforts and joined his forces with those of General Amaury Kruel on the outskirts of Rio de Janeiro.

In the early hours of Thursday, 2 April, the President of Congress, Auro Soares de Moura Andrade, managed to get the parliamentary majority to dismiss João Goulart, alleging that he had fled the country, and appointed the head of the Chamber of Deputies, Ranieri Mazzilli, as president. This was despite Goulart's allies in Congress questioning the veracity of the news of his fleeing and the legality of the dismissal itself.

The victorious rebels on 1 April 1964. From left to right: General Antônio Carlos da Silva Muricy, deputy José Maria Alkmin (dark suit), General Olímpio Mourão Filho and governor Magalhães Pinto. (*Journal do Brasil*)

The dismissed Goulart remained in Porto Alegre with General Argemiro de Assis Brasil, his ally and *aide-de-camp*, planning how to resist the coup with Leonel Brizola and General Ladário Teles, head of the Third Army based in Porto Alegre. However, Goulart wanted to avoid any fighting between Brazilian soldiers and be considered guilty of instigating a civil war, which was why he refused to ask the FAB to bomb the plotters or for sailors loyal to the government to advance on Rio de Janeiro to arrest the coup leaders. On the morning of 2 April, coup leader General Floriano Machado informed Goulart

Brigadier General Argemiro de Assis Brasil, Chief Minister of the Military House of the Presidency during the Goulart government. He accompanied the President into exile in Uruguay on 4 April 1964. When the general returned to Brazil, he presented himself to his superiors and was immediately arrested at Jurujuba Fort in Niterói. (Open source)

that the rebel troops had taken Curitiba without resistance and were heading to Porto Alegre, urging the ousted President to leave the country or risk being arrested.

Hearing this, Goulart fled to his family farm, located on the border with Uruguay, shortly before noon on 2 April. In the following hours, the coup definitively triumphed, without any movements emerging within the armed forces in defence of the deposed President. Goulart resisted the idea of leaving Brazil until his situation became untenable, and he was eventually forced to cross the Uruguayan border on 4 April.

The main Brazilian cities were occupied by armed soldiers, tanks and other military vehicles. In the city of Rio de Janeiro, the headquarters of the National Union of Students (*União Nacional dos Estudantes*, UNE) was burned down. The bases of associations that supported Goulart, including unions and the headquarters of political parties, were occupied by soldiers. Congress, under military pressure, appointed General Humberto de Alencar Castelo Branco as President of Brazil on 15 April 1964.

The conspirators set two basic objectives: in defence of the military institutions, to prevent the communists from taking political power in the country, and the establishment of an order to carry out profound legal reforms. The first objective was easy to achieve, but the second proved very difficult.

An Army M3 Scout Car passes near a column of M41 Walker Bulldog tanks in Rio de Janeiro during the 1964 coup (top). Army troops breaking up a demonstration in Porto Alegre on the day of the coup (bottom). (EFE; Open source)

The *De facto* Military Regimes

The coup of 1964 received broad support from private media outlets, such as *O Globo* and *Diario de Noticias*, as well as from a large part of the business community, rural landowners, part of the Catholic Church, several governors of important states (such as Carlos Lacerda from Guanabara, José de Magalhães Pinto from Minas Geráis and Ademar de Barros from São Paulo) and extensive sectors of the middle and upper-middle class. These media outlets had carried out a campaign to convince people that Goulart was leading Brazil towards a communist government similar to that of the Soviet Union and the People's Republic of China, while saying that 'what is good for the United States is good for Brazil'.[4] Landowners and businessmen also sought to control the economic crisis. Another enthusiastic supporter of the military regime was the US government under President Lyndon B. Johnson.

The fear of this tendency of the country towards the political Left was shared by the United States, whose government offered logistical support from its naval fleet in the Atlantic Ocean to assist the plotters in the event of armed resistance by Goulart or his allies against the rebellion. News of the coup was received with relief in Washington, where the government welcomed that the Brazilian military wanted more radical measures against subversion.

Within the Brazilian military establishment, two currents were soon revealed, one of them the so-called 'hard-liners', who had long favoured an authoritarian military regime. This radical group gathered around General Artur da Costa e Silva. There was also a more moderate group of officers who preferred a temporary authoritarian military government before a return to democracy. Among the latter was Marshal Castelo Branco. Both groups had in common opposition to communism and the implementation of profound economic and social reforms in Brazil. Nevertheless, the military installed a regime that superficially maintained previous democratic institutions, such as

Army troops being mobilised during the 1964 *coup d'état* (left). An M41 Walker Bulldog tank and a pair of Army jeeps in Brasília during the coup (right). (Open source)

General Humberto de Alencar Castelo Branco was appointed to occupy the Presidency after the 1964 *coup d'état*. (*Exército Brasileiro*)

Governors Carlos Lacerda from Guanabara, José de Magalhães Pinto from Minas Geráis and Ademar de Barros from São Paulo supported the military coup of 1964. (Open source)

United States President Lyndon B. Johnson, who was in office from 1963–1969. (White House Collection)

parliament and universal suffrage, but which prevented its detractors from exercising basic political rights (such as voting and being an electoral candidate) through decrees known as Institutional Acts.

Marshal Humberto de Alencar Castelo Branco (President 1964–1967)

Appointed Chief of Staff of the Brazilian Army by João Goulart in 1963, Castelo Branco was one of the leaders of the *coup d'état* in 1964. On 11 April, the Congress elected him as president by 361 votes, with 72 abstentions. He assumed power on 15 April immediately

Military Police deployed in Rio de Janeiro on 1 April 1964 during the coup. (Open source)

after the coup, and as soon as his mandate began, he dismantled the Left in Congress and established the abolition of political parties, in practice prohibiting them from carrying out activities, while imposing censorship of the press and other publications.

Castelo Branco assembled his cabinet with a combination of conservative politicians and technocrats. Its Minister of the Navy was Admiral Ernesto de Melo Batista and the Minister of Aeronautics was Air Lieutenant Brigadier Nelson Lavanére-Wanderley.

Gradually, starting the following year, the regime tightened. An Institutional Act made the presidential elections indirect, and politicians such as Juscelino Kubitschek, and even Carlos Lacerda and Adhemar de Barros – civilians who had supported the rebellion – were deprived of their political rights. Thereafter, elections for state governors by direct vote were prevented. Only two political parties were allowed: one supporting the government, the National Renewal Alliance (*Aliança Renovadora Nacional*, ARENA), and another in opposition, the Brazilian Democratic Movement (*Movimento Democrático Brasileiro*, MDB). The military leaders refrained from appointing a dictator with *caudillo* traits and preferred to establish a solid autocratic dominance over Brazilian politics, in alliance with many right-wing political leaders, increasingly suspending individual rights and freedoms. Meanwhile, opposition to the government grew, mainly from students and radical Left subversive groups, which would be the breeding ground for the appearance of the guerrilla movement.

The constitution of Brazil was suspended during Castelo Branco's *de facto* regime, being replaced in practice by Institutional Acts with the force of law, dictated by the armed forces. His government promoted economic and tax reforms, seeking greater state intervention in the economy. At the political level, Institutional Act No. 1, issued on 9 April 1964, suppressed the direct popular election of the President of the Republic, establishing that only Congress would have the power to elect the President. This same law also gave the government the ability to eliminate political rights for 10 years, thus allowing, for reasons of 'national security', more than a hundred opponents of the dictatorship to be expelled from their positions and prevented from participating in political activities. As a result of this, the vast majority of these opponents were left out of Congress and all Brazilian political life, and were therefore unable to help elect the President of the Republic.

The military government revived Brazil's relations with international financial institutions, which had been suspended since President Juscelino Kubitschek's decision in 1958 to reject the conditions

The President of Brazil, Marshal Castelo Branco (in a civilian suit), with his Minister of War, Army General Artur Costa e Silva, with binoculars, observing Army manoeuvres in the mid-60s. (Open source)

Marshal Humberto de Alencar Castelo Branco (third from the left in the front row) arriving at the Planalto Palace to be sworn in as President of the Republic on 15 April 1964. On the right, Castelo Branco receives the presidential sash after his oath. (Open source)

Military and police forces exercised tight control over Brazilian society and any attempt at public demonstration was harshly repressed. Many leftist leaders and students were arrested and even tortured. (Open source)

Above, Recife's Guararapes International Airport. Below left, one of the fatalities of the attack at the airport, the retired Admiral Nelson Gomes Fernandes. On the right, a wounded man, Colonel Sylvio Ferreira. (*Manchete* magazine)

imposed by the United States and the International Monetary Fund (IMF) for a $300 million loan. Economic measures criticised by the United States and the IMF were eliminated. Strikes were banned, unions were suppressed and real wages fell, with Gross Domestic Product (GDP) falling by seven percent in 1965. That same year, Brazil signed an agreement with the IMF, received new credits and its external debt was restructured by the United States, several European creditor countries and Japan. Annual loans rose from zero to an average of $73 million during the rest of the 1960s, and then to almost $500 million in the mid-1970s. The military regime's economic policy was praised by international financial institutions.

Ambitious projects were launched to integrate the Amazon into the national economy at the cost of environmental destruction and the displacement of indigenous populations. The most emblematic of these was the construction of a highway of more than 4,000km between the cities of Cabedelo in the northeast and Lábrea near the border with Bolivia. The project, which would never be fully completed, was inaugurated in 1972 with the aim of creating large agricultural holdings, better controlling the borders and bringing the poor to the new lands, avoiding agrarian reforms that the regime rejected.

In foreign policy, the regime supported Portuguese colonialism in Africa – which then included bloody conflicts in Guinea-Bissau, Angola and Mozambique – and developed trade relations with South Africa. In the 1960s, the only black government with which the regime maintained diplomatic relations was that of Houphouët-Boigny in Côte d'Ivoire/Ivory Coast.

Almost immediately after the coup, the police and armed forces began to arrest, torture and eliminate opponents identified as communists. Thousands of suspected people were arrested, but most were released within days or a few weeks. Those said to be directly involved in subversive activities spent a long time in prison, subjected to prolonged torture. A list was compiled of at least 5,000 'enemies of the state'. Furthermore, the new military regime suspended the political rights of 441 Brazilians, including former presidents (incredibly including Juscelino Kubitschek), governors and members of Congress, together with some diplomats, labour leaders, intellectuals and even public officials and military officers with sympathies towards the Left. A total of 421 military officers were forced to retire, among them 24 out of 91 with the rank of general. Between 1964 and 1966, it is believed that at least 5,000 people were taken into custody and 2,000 public employees were fired, having been accused of sympathising with socialism or communism. The crackdown also affected all union leaders, who were removed from their positions.

With the promotion of colonisation of indigenous peoples, those who resisted were arrested and taken to concentration camps, where many were murdered. This colonisation policy squandered natural resources, causing serious ecological damage in the Amazon area.

It was during Castelo Branco's term that terrorist attacks began to be carried out by various leftist groups. In February 1966, the US Consul's home in Porto Alegre was bombed. In July of that year, the USIS Library building in Brasília was hit, and also in that month, a bomb exploded at Recife's Guararapes Airport, targeting Minister of War General Costa e Silva, killing two people – a retired admiral and a journalist – and injuring 13 others. The minister's plane was diverted to another airport.

As the month of July 1966 approached and the term of Goulart's presidential term expired, Castelo Branco called for Congress to elect the new president, selected from a group of military leaders sympathetic to the regime. The election fell to General Artur da Costa e Silva, but it was agreed that Castelo Branco would extend his mandate to give time to develop the new Constitution of 1967, which was strongly authoritarian and concentrated the greatest number of governmental powers in the Executive Branch, reducing the influence

Remains of the Piper Aztec registration PP-ETT after the aerial collision in which former President Castelo Branco, his brother Cândido, writer Alba Frota, Army Major Manuel de Assis Nepomuceno and the pilot, Celso Tinoco, were killed. The only survivor was co-pilot Emílio Celso Tinoco. On the right, Castelo Branco's coffin was carried by an Army M113 to the cemetery in Rio de Janeiro. (*Folhapress*; Open source)

President Marshal Artur da Costa e Silva (fourth from the left in the front row) poses with his ministers on the day of the presidential inauguration on 15 March 1967. (Open source)

of the Legislative Branch. Right-wing politicians and jurists, as well as military leaders, intervened in support of this constitution.

After the approval of the constitution in the Brazilian parliament, which was dominated by right-wing allies of the armed forces, its entry into force was set for 15 March 1967, the date on which Castelo Branco left power to be succeeded by his Minister of War, the 'hard-liner' Marshal Costa e Silva. Just four months after leaving power, Castelo Branco died on 18 July at the age of 69 in a plane accident in Fortaleza, Brazil. The Piper PA-23-250 Aztec, registration PP-ETT, in which he was travelling collided with a Lockheed TF-33A, serial 4325, of the FAB. The Piper Aztec had entered the same flight altitude as four FAB TF-33As and collided with one of them, losing its vertical stabiliser, after which it entered into a flat spin and crashed. The TF-33A lost one of its tip tanks but was able to make an emergency landing.

Marshal Artur da Costa e Silva (President 1967–1969)

During his government, Costa e Silva aligned himself with the most conservative sectors of the Brazilian Right, maintaining that military control over national politics should remain for several years. Of the three military ministers, two were hard-liners: Admiral Augusto Hamann Rademaker from the Brazilian Navy (*Marinha do Brasil*, MB) and Air Marshal Márcio de Souza e Melo from the FAB. The new Minister of the Army was General Aurélio de Lyra Tavares and the head of the Military Presidential Staff was General Jayme Portella de Mello. Costa e Silva chose General Emílio Garrastazú Médici as Chief of the National Information Service (*Serviço Nacional de Informações*, SNI).

Although Costa e Silva promised to 'humanise' the revolution, social and subversive problems soon began to appear. Just a month after his rise to power, the Brazilian Army (*Exército Brasileiro*, EB) discovered a guerrilla training camp in Minas Geráis, and in June the Second Army headquarters in São Paulo was attacked by insurgents. Federal universities were considered hotbeds for recruiting subversives, so repressive action in them increased, especially in the Schools of Social Sciences and Humanities.

In March 1968, a confrontation between students and police in Rio de Janeiro resulted in the death of a student, Edson Luís de Lima Souto, who was killed by a police officer. The opposition now had a martyr that could mobilise anti-government sentiment. Subsequent protests against police violence and street riots, particularly a march by an estimated 100,000 people, generated virulent criticism in Congress from the opposition MDB against the regime. These parliamentary protests culminated in a request from opposition representative Márcio Moreira Alves to launch a boycott against the military celebrations of Brazil's independence on 7 September, in revenge for the government's refusal to stop police brutality against student demonstrations. Costa e Silva then requested that Congress lift the immunity of representative Moreira Alves from prosecution, but to the surprise of the public, Congress refused the presidential request on 11 December and insisted that only the parliamentary judge could prosecute Moreira Alves. The next day, Costa e Silva ordered the parliament to be closed by force

Edson Luís de Lima Souto, an 18-year-old high school student, was killed by the Military Police of Rio de Janeiro after a confrontation in downtown Rio on 28 March 1968. Edson was one of the first students to be killed by the Brazilian military government, and the aftermath of his death marked the beginning of a turbulent year for the regime. (Open source)

Marshal Artur Costa e Silva, President of Brazil from 1967–69. (Open source)

Presidents Costa e Silva and Johnson in Washington DC in 1967 (left). The visit of the British monarch, Queen Elizabeth II, to Brazil in 1968 (right). (Open source)

and suspended its functions indefinitely, evicting the congressmen gathered in Brasília with military personnel stationed inside the chambers. Mobilizations were not only carried out by the Left, as right-wing groups such as the Command for Hunting Communists (*Comando de Caça aos Comunistas*, CCC) and the Anti-Communist Movement (MAC) also demonstrated, attacking alleged 'left-wing targets' including theatre plays considered left-wing, and the School of Philosophy, without the police acting against the protesters. Urban and rural guerrilla movements emerged in the late 1960s as a consequence of the repressive military regime. Even though these guerrillas were considered a very low risk to the country, the military government justified the use of repressive force to crack down on them.

Meanwhile, the Brazilian economy enjoyed a strong industrial recovery in 1968 during Costa e Silva's government, led by transportation and electrical equipment production, and construction boomed. The balance of payment was also carried out successfully and inflation was contained.

In response to political tensions, Costa e Silva issued Institutional Act No. 5 on 13 December 1968, which granted almost all-encompassing powers to the President of Brazil, such as the power to close Congress, modify the prerogatives of public officials without expression of cause, and even dismiss them at the discretion of the President, in addition to suspending the rights of *habeas corpus*. Institutional Act No. 5 effectively suspended the recently promulgated Constitution of 1967, which despite being formulated in accordance with the request of the military regime itself, was less repressive. Due to social unrest, President Costa e Silva issued a decree placing all the state military and police forces under the control of the War Minister, and even the media were placed under the supervision of military courts.

A leftist attack on the São Paulo garrison headquarters in July 1969 caused the death of a soldier, precipitating a wave of arrests against suspected left-wing militants. Throughout 1969, Costa e Silva

President Costa e Silva passing by in an Army Dodge WC56 Command Car, saluting military chiefs prior to a military parade in Brasília in 1968. (Open source)

After the stroke suffered by President Costa e Silva, a military junta formed by General of the Army Aurélio de Lyra Tavares, Admiral of the Navy Augusto Rademaker and General of the Air Force Márcio Melo assumed leadership of the government (left), leaving aside Vice President Pedro Aleixo (right). (*Folhapress*)

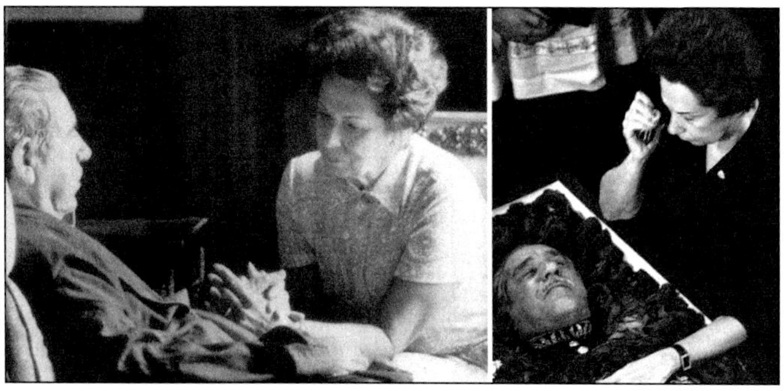

Following his stroke, President Costa e Silva was left paralysed on his right side. He is shown (left) being cared for by his wife, Iolanda. Costa e Silva died on 17 December 1969 (right). (Jader Neves/Manchete; *Folhapress*)

The facilities of Operation *Bandeirante*/OBAN in São Paulo. (Sergio Sade/Editora Abril)

planned to annul the very severe Institutional Act No. 5, formulating with various right-wing jurists and military leaders a project for a new constitution to replace that of 1967. The project was completed in August 1969. This new constitution was due to come into force on 7 September, but a week before that date, on 29 August, Costa e Silva suffered a stroke that left the right side of his body paralysed. Although he was able to hear and understand, he could not speak. Under these conditions, Costa e Silva could obviously not continue to govern, so the three military ministers removed him from office, temporarily replacing him with a military junta rather than the Vice President taking the reins, as stated in the Constitution of 1967. The junta comprised General of the Army Aurélio de Lyra Tavares, General of the Air Force Márcio Melo and Admiral of the Navy Augusto Rademaker. Costa e Silva's doctor had previously warned him about his high blood pressure and suggested that he rest and take things easy, but the President did not listen. He died on 17 December of that year.

Following Costa e Silva's initial inability to govern, and then his death, the military junta considered several military officers to succeed the President. Generals Afonso Albuquerque Lima, Aurélio Lyra Tavares, Antônio Carlos Muricy, Orlando Geisel and Syzeno Sarmento were all in the frame, but in the end the chosen candidate was General Emílio Garrastazú Médici, the Commander of the Third Army. Admiral Rademaker was selected as Vice President. At the same time, an amendment to the 1967 Constitution was approved, which increased the power of the President and established the strengthening of national security in the face of the guerrilla problem, even to the extent of declaring a state of siege. The guerrilla issue was not a huge problem, but its existence proved useful to justify repression. During its brief period in charge of the government, the military junta issued two Institutional Acts, Numbers 13 and 14. The first of these gave the government the power to permanently ban from the country any Brazilian citizen deemed to pose a danger to national security, and the second restored the death penalty in the case of foreign or subversive war. The Brazilian military was thus able to legally do whatever it wanted in the name of national security.

The so-called Operation Bandeirante (*Operação Bandeirante*, OBAN) had been launched on 1 July 1969. This was an information and investigation centre created by the Commander of the Second Army, General José Canavarro Pereira, and composed of members of the Army (2nd Military Region and 2nd Infantry Division), Air Force (4th Air Zone), Navy (6th Naval District), the Federal Police Department, the National Information Service and also government bodies of

The DOI-CODI facilities in Rio de Janeiro in 1970 (left). The officer in charge of DOI-CODI, Army Major Carlos Alberto Brilhante Ustra, was also known as *Doctor Tibiriçá* (right). (Fundo Ultima Hora)

General Emílio Garrastazú Médici assumed the Presidency of Brazil on 30 October 1969. (Open source)

Presidents Garrastazú Médici and Richard Nixon. The US government became a strong supporter of its Brazilian counterpart. (Open source)

the State of São Paulo (Secretariat of Public Security, Department of Political and Social Order (*Departamento Estadual de Ordem Política e Social,* DOPS), Public Force of the State of São Paulo and Civil Guard). OBAN was conceived to centralise and integrate the various military and police forces (information and political repression bodies), with the purpose of identifying, locating and capturing members of subversive groups that were operating in the area of the Second Army, particularly in São Paulo, consequently destroying or at least neutralising those organisations. The most notorious member of OBAN was Major Carlos Alberto Brilhante Ustra. OBAN's structure was based on three axes, radiating from the Coordination Centre:

- Information Centre, responsible for examining and processing raw data from reports.
- Operations Centre, in charge of combat actions.
- Diffusion Centre, responsible for psychological action and control of news linked to internal security.

Without formal or legal ties, OBAN was in essence a paramilitary formation for direct and violent action outside the law, which gave it agility and brutal effectiveness through the use of torture. In 1970, OBAN, although still known as such, had officially become the Detachment of Internal Operations-Operational Command of Internal Defence (*Destacamento de Operações Internas-Comando Operacional de Defesa Interna*, DOI-CODI) of the Second Army. By placing it under the jurisdiction of DOI-CODI, the intention was to reduce its autonomy, but in practice this did not happen. In 1970, the person in charge of DOI-CODI was Carlos Alberto Brilhante Ustra, an Army artillery major, also known in torture circles by the codenames *Major*, *Doctor Silva* and *Doctor Tibiriçá*. Ustra headed DOI-CODI until 1974, being succeeded until 1976 by Major Audir Santos Maciel.

Army General Emílio Garrastazú Médici (President 1969–1974)

Emílio Garrastazú Médici had been a low profile military officer, virtually unknown to the public before he became the President of Brazil. He had been Costa e Silva's Chief of Staff in the late 1950s. Later he served as military attaché in Washington during Castelo Branco's government and then was appointed Chief of the SNI. After becoming a four-star general, he was named Commander of the Third Army in Rio Grande do Sul.

For the purpose of inaugurating his mandate on 30 October 1969, Médici requested the reopening of Congress, which he achieved despite the fact that almost a year earlier his predecessor had forcibly dissolved it. Despite this initial gesture, Médici devoted most of his efforts to severely repressing left-wing opposition to his regime. Faced with the emergence of a leftist urban guerrilla movement in Brazil, Médici ordered the use of espionage and torture to suppress the movement, with the help of an intelligence service led by General Orlando Geisel. The reinforcement of political repression during his government made the Médici period known as the 'leaden years' of the military regime.

Richard Nixon's administration in the US became a strong supporter of the Médici regime, not only for its economic success but also its anti-communist credentials. President Médici visited Washington DC in December 1971 and was given a state dinner at the White House.

Although Médici refrained from dismissing public officials en masse in accordance with the powers granted to him by the Institutional Acts, he maintained tight control over the press and political activity, highlighting the massive use of propaganda to sustain popular support for the military regime. Even the 1970 FIFA soccer World Cup won by Brazil was used by Médici to launch a campaign of persecutions and arrests against leftist militants, while some years later nationalist and patriotic propaganda was manipulated to impose loyalty to the military regime, identifying this with loyalty to the nation itself. It was

The famous Brazilian soccer player Edson Arantes do Nacimento, known as Pelé, hugs President Garrastazú Médici in Brasília after winning the 1970 FIFA soccer World Cup. (O Cruzeiro)

The progressive Catholic Archbishop Helder Cámara of Recife, a harsh critic of military governments (left). The conservative Catholic Archbishop Geraldo Proença Sigaud of Diamantina, who had a marked anti-communist tendency (right). (Open source)

The Minister of Finance, Delfim Netto (on the right with glasses), and his economic team, who achieved the so-called 'Brazilian miracle'. Delfim Netto was Minister of Finance from 1967–1974, then Minister of Agriculture in 1979 and finally Minister of Planning between 1979 and 1985 (*Folhapress*).

The slogans of the Brazilian Economic Miracle: 'Love Brazil or leave it' and 'No one can be safer in this country'. (Open source)

also in that year that a combine military and police force launched *Operação Gaiola* (Operation Birdcage), when hundreds of people, mainly union leaders and university students, were arrested in just two weeks.

Other instances of opposition to the military regimes were the Bar Association and the Catholic Church. Lawyers presented legal appeals in defence of people who had justly or unjustly been detained. In the case of the Catholic Church, the Brazilian bishops were divided among progressives like the Recife Archbishop Helder Cámara, and moderates and conservatives such as Archbishop Geraldo Proença Sigaud. The progressive clergy supported various Catholic movements such as Popular Action (*Ação Popular*, AP), Catholic University Youth (*Juventude Universitária Católica*, JUC), Catholic Working Youth (*Jeunesse ouvrière chrétienne*, JOC) and other groups that were leaning towards the Left, from which several subversives would eventually emerge. Meanwhile, the conservative bishops supported the military government and were openly opposed to the insurgent threat in Brazil. The progressive bishops were accused of helping the subversives, but the National Conference of Bishops of Brazil (*Conferência Nacional dos Bispos do Brasil*, CNBB) rejected the charge. The security forces often raided convents, churches and Catholic schools and universities in search of hidden subversives. Nevertheless, the Catholic Church proved a thorn on the side of the Médici government.

On the economic level, Médici promoted massive public works projects, taking advantage of the ease of obtaining money loans internationally in the early 1970s. The construction of housing for the working class and state subsidies to industry promoted a 'Brazilian miracle' characterised by sustained growth of the economy and an increase in the GDP to levels not previously known, indirectly causing an increase in the middle class and greater spending on consumer goods. Many previously unemployed workers found jobs in the booming industry and public works. Somehow, the temporary economic boom legitimised the military regime in the eyes of the middle and upper classes. Brazil's GDP rose at an annual rate of 10.9 percent from 1968–1974, while industry grew by 12.6 percent per year, the automobile industry being the most dynamic with annual growth of 34.5 percent. Meanwhile, inflation was kept between 15.7 and 17 percent, but above all, Brazil's foreign exchange reserves increased from US$656 million in 1969 to US$6,417 million in 1973. These economic results gave the government a level of relative popular acceptance, despite its ferocious censorship, repression and constant violation of human rights.

In 1973, the military regime managed to complete an agreement with Paraguay for the construction of the gigantic Itaipú Dam, securing an energy source that would sustain the industrial and commercial expansion of the richest regions in southern Brazil. Likewise, state-owned companies such as Petrobrás, the Brazilian oil company, increased their power and influence in Brazil's economy.

Despite favourable economic indicators, the Brazilian miracle did not survive the global 1973 oil crisis, leaving a legacy of external debt, excessive public spending and an overloaded and inefficient state apparatus. The following economic depression caused greater havoc among the poorer classes that depended on state economic activity. This increased the inequality between rich and poor, being one of the highest such levels in the world and increased extreme poverty that was then concentrated not only in the countryside, but in the *favelas* (slums) of the nation's large cities.

Regarding foreign policy, in 1971, Médici strongly backed Richard Nixon's government in the United States in its attempts to overthrow Chilean President Salvador Allende, supporting the idea that after Allende's deposition a *de facto* government would be installed in Chile. In 2011, secret files from the Brazilian intelligence services were declassified, which stated that, 'If the United States government did not support the *coup d'état* to overthrow the Chilean Marxist government, the government of Brazil would do so and that the coup in Chile was going out yes or yes.'[5] In other files, it was indicated that:

> Brazil will be in charge of supporting the Chilean government in the face of the international political-diplomatic offensive against it that aims to isolate Chile in every way, for this Brazil will occupy all its power to neutralize Chile's enemies in the votes of international forums, it will also provide it with soft credits that will allow it to resist the pressing situation in which it currently finds itself since the international isolation after the overthrow of the Marxist government has revealed an economic crisis that affects our ally as a result of the nationalization of the economy by the deposed regime. Added to this is the fact that Chile is threatened by its three neighbours (Argentina, Peru and Bolivia), so the credits will be to alleviate the economy, [with] access to products in the international market (when Brazilian industry is not capable of providing them).[6]

Another declassified document reads, 'We must increase the quotas for Chileans in the National Information Service or Brazil unconditionally trusts and supports the Chilean military government because in Chile, like in Brazil, the military is serious and if they have decided to come to power it is because the situation was insurmountable and they are restoring the destroyed institutions.'[7] These files are just some of many more that confirm Brazil was the most important ally of the Chilean military government, even more so than the United States, which from 1978 opposed the Chilean regime.

Médici left power on 15 March 1974, General Ernesto Geisel having been elected the new President of Brazil the previous year. Médici died of a stroke in 1985 in Rio de Janeiro.

Army General Ernesto Geisel (President 1974–1979)

In 1973, President Médici nominated Geisel as the presidential candidate of ARENA, the party sponsored by the armed forces for the Presidency of Brazil. Geisel won the election by vote of Parliament and assumed presidential command on 15 March 1974 for a five-year term. Geisel was Brazil's first Lutheran president, a son of German immigrants. He was a perfectionist in administrative details and lacked the typical Brazilian charm in public life. Geisel's first objective was to

In 1973, President Garrastazú Médici met with his successor, General Ernesto Geisel. (Open source)

President General Ernesto Geisel on 15 March 1974, the day of his inauguration. (Open source)

slowly modify Brazil's system of repression by reducing power of the military hard-liners in order to re-democratise the country.

At that time, the Brazilian economy was suffering the serious aftereffects of the 1973 oil crisis, as a result of which Brazil's external debt was progressively increasing. Faced with this situation, Geisel sought new economic opportunities for Brazil in terms of foreign policy, establishing diplomatic relations and economic ties with the People's Republic of China and Angola. This approach was due to the regime's marked pragmatism; its alliance with the United States remained in force in the context of the Cold War, and this new policy did not mean any alteration in the marked anti-communism of Geisel and his government. Geisel's desire to establish commercial and economic ties with countries in Africa and Europe was due to a desire to avoid permanent unconditional alignment with the United States and to obtain new alternatives for economic cooperation favourable to Brazil.

Geisel also began a timid attempt at democratisation and the political opening of the regime, even while maintaining the tight control of the armed forces over political life. Geisel and his advisors seemed to understand that the armed forces could not exercise political tutelage over Brazil in perpetuity, which was why it was necessary to return power to civilian politicians, meanwhile trying to avoid any concessions to the Brazilian Left and preventing open criticism of the military. In 1976, he tried to limit the possibility of the opposition MDB obtaining a massive victory in Parliament like the one achieved in 1974, for fear that the government would lose its parliamentary majority. In view of this, Geisel approved a new censorship law in April 1977 that increased restrictions on freedom of expression and even prohibited opposition candidates from making public speeches, requiring them to publicise only their name and application number.

At the end of 1976, right-wing terrorism had broken out in Brazil. A bomb exploded at the Rio headquarters of the Brazilian Press Association, and there were also bomb attacks and telephone threats aimed at notable clerical critics of the government, with in one instance

President Geisel visited Paraguay in December 1975. Paraguayan President General Alfredo Stroessner is reading a welcome speech at Asunción International Airport. (Author's archives)

There was a cooling of relations between Brazil and the United States during the Jimmy Carter government, due to Brazil being included in the list of countries that did not respect human rights. (*O Globo* archives)

Brothers Orlando (1905–1979) and Ernesto (1907–1996) Beckmann Geisel had a long military career in the Brazilian Army. Ernesto became the President of Brazil and Orlando was Minister of the Army in the Garrastazú Médici government, both with the rank of army general. (*Exército Brasileiro*)

President Geisel with his successor, Figueiredo. (*Veja* magazine)

a bishop being kidnapped and beaten. The group behind these attacks was the Brazilian Anti-Communist Alliance, an organisation similar to the Triple A in neighbouring Argentina.[8]

Once the Democrat Jimmy Carter assumed the Presidency of the United States and announced a campaign in favour of human rights worldwide, Brazil was included in the blacklist of countries that violated those rights. The Geisel administration received the news with fury and responded by cancelling American military aid agreements that had been in effect since 1952, as well as other arrangements.

However, in 1978 Geisel annulled Institutional Act No. 5, one of the most repressive regulations that had been approved by the military government in December 1968. Before finishing his term in office, Geisel managed to have another military man who followed his ideas elected as his successor, General João Baptista de Oliveira Figueiredo. Geisel died from cancer in Rio de Janeiro in 1996.

Army General João Baptista de Oliveira Figueiredo (President 1979–1985)

Figueiredo assumed the Presidency of Brazil on 15 March 1979. He continued the gradual process of 'opening' (democratisation) begun in 1974, appointing liberal technocrats in all the ministries. An amnesty law signed by Figueiredo on 28 August 1979 granted total amnesty to not only those convicted of 'political or related' crimes between 1961 and 1978 (except for those found guilty of acts of terrorism and armed resistance to the government), but also to military and police forces, to free them from prosecution in the future.

Presidential inauguration on 15 March 1979 of Army General João Baptista de Oliveira Figueiredo, who is being embraced by his predecessor, Ernesto Geisel. (Open source)

Two key politicians of the so-called democratic 'opening' initiated by the government of General Figueiredo: Luíz Inácio 'Lula' da Silva (left), founder of the Workers' Party (PT), and Leonel Brizola (right), founder of the Democratic Labour Party (PDT) in 1979. (Open source)

One of the most infamous detectives of the Civil Police was Sérgio Paranhos Fleury (1933–1979), who participated in the capture, torture and death of numerous subversives when he acted as a delegate of the Department of Political and Social Order (DOPS) of São Paulo. (Open source)

General João Baptista de Oliveira Figueiredo held high positions in the military regimes. He was Minister-Chief of the Military Cabinet from 1969–1974, head of the SNI from 1974–1978, and between 1979 and 1985 held the Presidency of the Republic, being the last military leader of the country. (Open source).

The new government tried to avoid further repression and many political exiles were able to return to Brazil. One of the most infamous torturers of the military regimes was detective Sérgio Paranhos Fleury, who had planned the ambush and subsequent murder of leading left-wing activist Carlos Marighella, the murder of the militant Joaquim Cámara, and who also had carried out hundreds of interrogations and tortures of political prisoners and subversives. In 1979, he had bought a yacht and was planning a sea voyage when he slipped off the deck and fell into the water. Although he was rescued immediately, he suffered a devastating heart attack and died.

In the early 1980s, the military regime was unable to effectively maintain the two-party system established in 1966. The Figueiredo administration dissolved the government-controlled party, ARENA, and allowed new parties to form. Leonel Brizola founded the Democratic Labour Party (*Partido Democrático Trabalhista*, PDT) and Luiz Inácio 'Lula' da Silva created the Workers' Party (*Partido dos Trabalhadores*, PT) in 1979. In 1981, Congress issued a law restoring direct elections for state governors. The legislative elections of Monday, 15 November 1982 brought victory to ARENA's successor, the pro-government PDS, with 43.22 percent of the votes, while the opposition Brazilian Democratic Movement Party (*Partido do Movimento Democrático Brasileiro*, PMDB) gained 42.96 percent.

The government of three large states – São Paulo, Rio de Janeiro and Minas Geráis – was won by the opposition. However, political developments were overshadowed by economic problems such as inflation and unemployment. Furthermore, the nation's external debt grew uncontrollably, reaching massive proportions, making

In the period between 1964 and 1985 there were five military governments in Brazil. From left to right: Presidents Castelo Branco, Costa e Silva, Garrastazú Médici, Geisel and Figueiredo. (Open source)

President José Sarney, originally the Vice President to Neves, assumed the Presidency following the illness and death of President-elect Tancredo Neves (left). President-elect Tancredo Neves, who did not manage to assume the Presidency due to his illness (right). (Open source)

Brazil one of the largest debtors in the world, owing a figure close to US$90 billion.

The austerity program imposed by the government did not bring signs of recovery for the Brazilian economy until the end of the Figueiredo period. The President was often incapacitated by illness and took two extended terms of leave to treat his health in 1981 (the year in which he suffered a heart attack) and 1983, but civilian Vice President Antonio Aureliano Chaves de Mendonça did not enjoy great political power.

Since the 1964 *coup d'état*, Brazilians had not been allowed to vote to directly elect the President, but in 1983 they began to demonstrate for a return to democracy through the *Diretas Já* (Direct Voting Now) movement. The opposition fought vigorously to pass a constitutional amendment to allow popular elections in November 1984, but Figueiredo was against this move and in that year Congress rejected the return of direct elections. However, the opposition, led by Tancredo Neves, won the presidential election in the electoral college on 15 January 1985, gaining 480 votes out of 686, thus ending the military regimes. Figueiredo retired after the end of his term and died on 24 December 1999 at the age of 81.

President-elect Tancredo Neves publicly opposed any attempt to try military or police officers accused of torture and other human rights violations. His main objective was the reconciliation of Brazilian society.

Due to serious intestinal problems, Tancredo Neves had to undergo several medical treatments. On the eve of being sworn in, he could no longer bear the pain, being admitted to hospital in Brasília for urgent surgery. Vice President José Sarney was sworn in as Provisional President until the recovery of Tancredo Neves. However, the President's delicate state of health continued and he had to be transferred by air to the leading specialist hospital in São Paulo, where he underwent seven operations and was kept alive under intensive care. He eventually passed away on 21 April of that year. A few days before, and with the knowledge that Tancredo Neves would never recover from his terminal illness, José Sarney was sworn in as President for the period 1985–1990.

2
SUBVERSIVE GROUPS IN BRAZIL

Urban and rural subversion and guerrilla warfare slowly emerged from political parties and leftist movements in Brazil that, due to violent repression by the state, went underground after the 1964 coup. It was this very leftist movement that questioned why there was little or no resistance when the 'fascistic' military took power, sponsored by 'imperialists'.

The first political party that was repressed was the Brazilian Communist Party (*Partido Comunista Brasileiro*, PCB), whose leaders strictly followed Moscow's instructions and whose 'official' line of action was to come to power through democratic elections. That aim would cause a schism with their pro-Chinese faction, who openly supported an armed struggle. The latter finally deserted from the PCB, and together with Trotskyist and radical Catholic Church groups formed the backbone of the armed resistance to the military regimes of Brazil. Between 1964 and 1967, they carried out a series of terrorist attacks, for example the non-fatal bombings of the Peace Corps office in Rio de Janeiro and the US Air Force attaché's home in Rio, but they were still considered only a nuisance and not a major threat to the government.

In the mid-1960s, there were several subversive groups carrying out actions against the military regime, but they were far from united. The groups all acted independently and in uncoordinated fashion in small cells, just to avoid being captured, so their attacks proved ineffective. Nevertheless, they had some successes, such as robbing poorly guarded banks in order to steal money to finance their fight. Some of these groups received urban guerrilla training in North Korea, China and Cuba. Like all subversive groups in Latin America, those in Brazil also hoped to get the support of the 'oppressed population' and the 'proletarians', but they were never able to achieve this, since the common citizens in the cities and the peasants in the countryside were afraid of military and police repression or were simply not convinced by the ideology and actions that the guerrillas proclaimed.

Towards the end of the 1960s, the government, starting to become seriously concerned about insurgents, began a broad campaign of

The leader of the MRT, Francisco Julião (above left). VARIG Airlines Boeing 707-441, registration PP-VJB (above right). Below, the remains of the VARIG Boeing after the accident in Peru. (Open source; Rubens Martins Borges Filho; Open Source)

arrests of people suspected of being involved not only in demonstrations but also in terrorist attacks. Torture had been a police tool in Brazil since the 1930s, its use to obtain data being considered normal practice, but the military also began to use it in their intelligence work. Thus, in June 1969, OBAN was launched, a joint action between the police and the Army, initially only in São Paulo but later extended to many other cities. It consisted of the arrest of thousands of people to check their documents, an intimidating measure intended to ensure that the general population did not support the subversives. Nevertheless, several subversive groups operated to varying degrees in Brazil in the 1960s and 1970s during the *de facto* military regimes.

Tiradentes Revolutionary Movement (*Movimento Revolucionário Tiradentes*, MRT)

The MRT was a clandestine political group linked to the *Ligas Camponesas* (Peasant Leagues) that was founded in Ouro Preto on 21 April 1962 by Francisco Julião. Under the influence of the Cuban Revolution, with members of the Leagues, it aimed for a socialist revolution with peasant bases in Brazil. The movement was a precursor to the left-wing armed struggle in Brazil and one of the first attempts to start a rural guerrilla movement, an ambition that would only be effectively implemented years later with the *Guerrilha do Araguaia*.

The MRT began purchasing ranches to use as training camps for guerrilla fighters. Eight rural guerrilla bases were created, among which the one at Dianópolis in Goiás (currently Rio da Conceição in Tocantins) was discovered by government forces at the end of 1962. The other bases were at Gibués in Piauí, Itanhém in Bahía, Rio Preto in Rio de Janeiro, Prudentópolis in Paraná, São João dos Patos in Maranhão and one on the border with Bolivia in Acre.

At the beginning of the 1960s, the Peasant Leagues had radicalised their position, intending to inspire a revolution in the countryside. Events in Cuba led to a questioning of the theses of the PCB, which was against the use of an armed struggle. With the training of militants and possible financing by Cuba, the guerrilla camps were implemented at the end of 1961. Francisco Julião, the best-known representative of the Leagues, did not have direct participation in the guerrilla, whose main leader was Clodomir Santos de Morais.

Militants of the Tiradentes Revolutionary Movement (MRT). Clockwise from upper left: Devanir José de Carvalho, Joaquim Alencar de Seixas, Aderval Alves Coqueiro and Dimas Antônio Casemiro. (Open source)

The militants spent a year in the camps, dispersed across all regions of Brazil, but there was little effective military preparation due to internal disputes and lack of resources. Security agencies monitored their movements and the Army, supported by the government of Goiás, dismantled the Dianópolis cell at the end of 1962, capturing not only its leaders but also weapons and ammunition. During the same period, Clodomir de Morais was arrested and documents linking Cuba to the guerrillas were found in the wreckage of VARIG Boeing 707-441, registration PP-VJB, Flight RG810, which crashed during its approach to Lima International Airport in Peru, with the death of all 80 passengers and 17 crew members on board. The guerrilla project, which was already weak, thus ended in failure.

Despite its small size, the guerrilla attempt was covered in the national press, was taken seriously by authorities in the United States and contributed to the decline of the Peasant Leagues. The first attempt at rural guerrilla warfare was thus dismantled before its actions against the state could begin.

Between 1969 and 1971, another Marxist-Leninist, revolutionary and anti-imperialist movement with the same name was formed, bringing together a group centred around Devanir José de Carvalho and Plínio Petersen Pereira. It was dubbed the Tiradentes Revolutionary Movement in homage to the previous group and was linked to the Camponesa Leagues, which operated between 1961 and 1962, so as to confuse attempts to repress its activities. Among its main actions were the robbery of an armoured car belonging to the Brink's security transport company – considered one of the most profitable actions of the armed struggle in Brazil – and the murder of businessman Henning Albert Boilesen in reprisal for the killing of Devanir de Carvalho, when the organisation was in its early stages. The MRT was dismantled through state repression in April 1971 following a series

The subversive group Popular Action was formed from the Catholic University Youth groups (JUC), which soon broke away from their Christian principles to adopt an extreme leftist line. (Open source)

Lawyer Aldo da Silva Arantes, who became the leader of Popular Action in 1965 (left). Jaor Ferreira de Sá led the *Ação Popular Marxista Leninista* in the 1970s (right). (Open source; Centro Sérgio Buarque de Holanda)

of arrests of former militants, from whom information extracted by torture produced a domino effect among members of the organisation that led to the end of its activities.

Popular Action (*Ação Popular*, AP)

Ação Popular was a leftist organisation, created in June 1962, following a congress in Belo Horizonte, the result of several meetings of the JUC and other associations. At its second congress, held in Salvador in 1963, AP decided to press for 'humanist socialism', seeking ideological inspiration in Emmanuel Mounier and Jesuits such as Teilhard de Chardin and Henrique Cláudio de Lima Vaz. It was mainly composed of student leaders, among whom were Herbert José de Sousa (the group's leader between 1963 and 1965), Jair Ferreira de Sá, José Serra, Vinícius Caldeira Brant and Aldo Arantes (leader from 1965 onwards).

The emergence of AP resulted from the politicisation of the JUC, which began between 1959 and 1960. Despite not having a large number of militants, the JUC was, like the communist PCB, a very organised student force. Until 1959, the JUC developed activities of a markedly religious and internal nature, with interest in underlying political problems. However, from that year on, it turned towards political and social issues. This caused a violent reaction both within and outside the university environment. The JUC later came to be denounced as a communist organisation under a Catholic façade. The group thus began to represent the Catholic Left within the student movement. The hierarchy of the Brazilian Catholic Church spoke out on the matter, stating that the JUC did not represent authentic Christian thought and that it was highly politicised with left-wing ideas.

After the 1964 coup, AP radicalised towards the extreme Left and abandoned its Christian principles. In 1965, a resolution was adopted that openly formulated the objective of seizing power by insurrection, through the strategy of the Socialist Revolution of National Liberation. At that time, Aldo da Silva Arantes became the group's new General Coordinator, replacing Betinho, who had been elected in 1963. AP began publishing a new monthly newspaper, *Revolução* (Revolution). In 1966, AP once again became the dominant force of the UNE, whose president was José Serra. AP concentrated its actions in the Rio de Janeiro–Minas Geráis–São Paulo triangle and, being pro-Chinese, was in favour of forming a 'liberation army' to seize political power in Brazil.

Using the influence of the Chinese Revolution, AP adopted a line of proletarianisation of its members, which consisted of placing militants in factories and in close contact with peasants. As in any leftist organisation, an internal struggle began within the AP, led by the Maoist Jair Ferreira de Sá. In 1968, this internal struggle resulted in the formation of a dissident group, the Workers' Revolutionary Party (*Partido Revolucionário dos Trabalhadores*, PRT), directed by the Catholic Father Alípio de Freitas, Vinícius Caldeira Brant and Altino Dantas. The PRT subsequently approached the Marxist Revolutionary Organisation – Operative Politics (*Organização Revolucionária Marxista – Política Operária*, POLOP) and the 8 October Revolutionary Movement (*Movimento Revolucionário 8 de Outubro*, MR-8). In 1980, several former members of the PRT participated directly in the creation of the Workers' Party (*Partido dos Trabalhadores*, PT).

Starting in 1971, there was a further split in the AP, forming two factions. One went by the name Marxist Leninist Popular Action (*Ação Popular Marxista Leninista*, APML), and was the larger group, led by Duarte Pereira, Haroldo Lima, Aldo Arantes and José Renato Rabelo, which was closer to the PCdoB and would eventually join it. The smaller faction, led by Jair Ferreira de Sá, Paulo Wright and Manoel da Conceição, was known as the Socialist AP. The APML eventually relented and accepted the PCdoB as the only revolutionary party, adopting its doctrinal lines of unrestricted Stalinism, which became the common ideological thread of both organisations and characterised Brazilian society and the Brazilian revolution. The merger took place in May 1973.

After the merger of the largest APML group with the PCdoB, the minority faction of the APML, still experiencing the effects of a deep political and ideological crisis, was practically dismantled by the brutal repression unleashed by the infiltration of former militant Gilberto Prata Soares, after whose reintegration into the group there were several militants killed. A final faction of the APML survived the repression that would last until the early 1980s, when it dissolved. Many of the members of this faction joined the forces that founded the PT, where they met with other militants from the progressive sectors of the Catholic Church, whose origins also went back to the JUC and with whom they had never lost contact.

On 25 July 1966, an autonomous command belonging to AP carried out the attack on Guararapes Airport in Recife, which targeted General

Costa e Silva, the Minister of War elected by the military to be the next President of the Republic. The attack killed the secretary of the Government of Pernambuco, Edson Régis de Carvalho, and reserve Admiral Nelson Gomes Fernandes, and 15 other people were wounded. The result of this action within AP was the immediate dissolution of parallel armed commands. The National Directorate, which had no knowledge of the attack, condemned the action. Furthermore, the militants involved in the attack were condemned to 'ideological re-education'. Internally, the main result of the attack was the abandoning of the organisation of urban armed actions.

National Liberation Action (*Ação Libertadora Nacional*, ALN)

The ALN was a guerrilla group active during the military regimes in Brazil between 1964 and 1985. The ALN had its origins in the expulsion of former deputy Carlos Marighella from the PCdoB in 1967 due to his attendance at a conference of the Latin American Solidarity Organisation (*Organización Latinoamericana de Solidaridad*, OLAS) in Havana, Cuba. Marighella was a tall, muscular Bahian and had been a PCB member since the mid-1930s.

The group began to take shape in 1964, describing its ideology as 'Eclectic-Marxism' criticising the Brazilian upper class. The ALN was the most structured organisation of the urban guerrilla and was also the one in which the number of women involved was proportionally greater than any other organisation. Its ideals were the fight against the military regime and the installation of a popular revolutionary government, the same objectives as the other two groups that initiated armed actions against the military regimes, the MR-8 and the Brazilian Revolutionary Communist Party (*Partido Comunista Brasileiro Revolucionário*, PCBR).

US Army Captain Charles Rodney Chandler was killed by the ALN. (Open source)

ALN emblem (left). Carlos Marighella, originally leader of the PCB, later in the ALN. (Open source)

The ALN attacked the Second Army Headquarters in São Paulo with a van full of explosives. (Open source)

In its program of action, ALN members defined themselves as 'guerrillas, terrorists and burglars' rather than men who depended on the votes of other revolutionaries or anyone else to fulfil their duty. They stated that democratic centralism did not apply to revolutionary organisations like the ALN.

The ALN proposed objective and immediate action to annihilate the military regime, defending armed struggle, guerrilla and popular war as instruments of political action. A dissident group formed around Marighella calling itself the Communist Group of São Paulo/Ala Marighella (*Agrupamento Comunista de São Paulo*), while recruiting more militants who left the Communist Party. To finance its operations, the ALN dedicated itself to robbing banks, money transported in trucks and even a train that transported money, in 1968 and 1969 in the São Paulo area. They also robbed weapons, ammunition and explosives from Rochester Industries at Mogi das Cruzes in the State of São Paulo, and several gun stores.

On 22 June 1968, ALN members disguised as soldiers stole weapons and ammunition from the Army Hospital in São Paulo and then planned an assault on the Second Army Headquarters. A van full of dynamite was prepared to explode at the main gate of the military base, but the vehicle collided with the perimeter wall. When a guard went to inspect, the dynamite charge exploded, killing him instantly and injuring six other military personnel.

On 12 October 1968, the ALN murdered in cold blood Captain Charles Rodney Chandler, a member of the US Army who was a sociology student at the Armando Álvares Penteado Foundation in São Paulo. They believed that Chandler was an undercover Central Intelligence Agency (CIA) agent and that he had tortured members of the Viet Cong during his service in Vietnam.

Most of the group's activists were students, who constituted the front-line of the organisation. Of the four kidnappings of diplomats carried out in the country's history, the ALN participated in the execution of two of them. The first, carried out with the MR-8, was that of American Ambassador Charles Burke Elbrick on 4 September

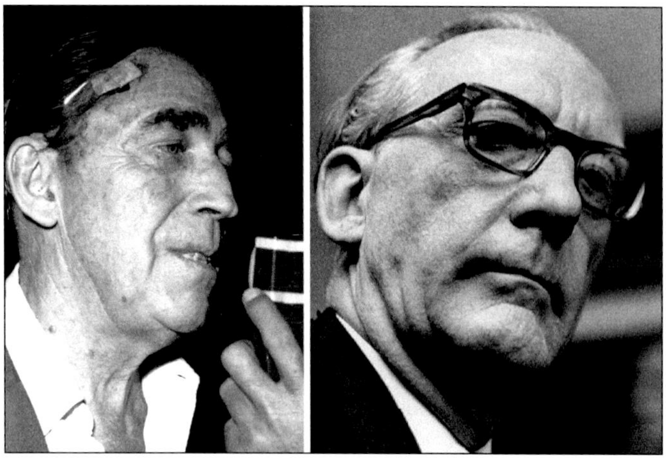

The US Ambassador to Brazil, Charles Burke Elbrick, was kidnapped by the ALN on 4 September 1969 (left). The Ambassador of the Federal Republic of Germany to Brazil, Ehrenfried von Holleben, was also kidnapped by the ALN (right). (Open source)

Above, the subversive Carlos Marighella was killed by government forces in an ambush organised by detective Sérgio Paranhos Fleury in São Paulo in 1969. Below, the group of political prisoners released and exiled to Algeria to free the kidnapped German Ambassador. (Open source)

1969, through which they managed to free 15 political prisoners, in addition to gaining great prominence in the press, publicising the organisation's acronym and the idea of armed struggle. The second kidnapping was that of German Ambassador Ehrenfried von Holleben, which forced the regime to release 44 political prisoners. Meanwhile, Marighella was murdered in an ambush organised by police chief Sérgio Paranhos Fleury, one of the main torturers of the military regime, on 4 November 1969 in the Casa Branca shopping centre in São Paulo. His successor was Joaquim Cámara Ferreira, known

Above, *Cruzeiro do Sul* Airlines Sud Aviation SE-210 Caravelle VI-R registration PP-PDX. Below, the aircraft was surrounded by FAB troops and covered in smoke and foam before the passengers and crew were rescued and the insurgents captured. (Hélio Bastos Salmon; *Folhapress*)

as *El Viejo* (Old Man) or *Toledo*, a journalist and former member of the PCB since the 1940s. Ferreira led the ALN until he was arrested by the police and tortured to death by Commissioner Fleury on 23 October 1970, following information obtained under torture from the guerrilla José Tavares, known as *Severino*.

In 1970, Eduardo Collen Leite, known as *Bacuri*, an important member of the ALN, was arrested by Fleury's team and died after 109 days of confinement and torture. His body, found on the coast at São Sebastião in São Paulo state, was delivered to his family in a sealed coffin, in an attempt to hide what he had suffered at the hands of his torturers.

On 1 July 1970, four ALN subversives – Fernando Palha Freire, his brother Eiraldo Palha Freire, Colombo Vieira de Souza and Jessie Jane – posed as ordinary passengers to board the Cruzeiro do Sul Airlines Sud Aviation SE-210 Caravelle VI-R, registration PP-PDX, for Flight 105 from Rio de Janeiro to Buenos Aires, with a stop in São Paulo. The aircraft was piloted by Captain Harro Cyranka and carried a total of 31 passengers and seven crew members. Before take-off, the four hijackers took control of the aircraft by entering the flight deck. Through the aircraft's radio, they demanded the release of their imprisoned comrades, including Jessie's father, and that they be sent to Cuba. FAB troops immediately surrounded the Caravelle and shot out its tires to prevent the aircraft from taking off. The aircraft was then covered in smoke and foam to allow commando troops to storm the aircraft, wounding Eiraldo Freire – who would later die at the FAB hospital – and capturing the other three hijackers. The Caravelle was repaired and flew again, but on 1 June 1973, during its final approach to São Luis Airport, it crashed, killing 27 people on board.

A Catholic anti-communist demonstration in Brazil in the 1960s. The main banner reads: 'Brazil will not be a new Cuba' (left). Brazilian anti-communist pamphlets: 'Do you know that Communism wants to enslave the world?' (top). 'Communism is like this: Communism despises your religion' (bottom). (Open source)

In 1971, a group of dissidents who had undergone guerrilla training in Cuba created the Popular Liberation Movement (*Movimento de Libertação Popular,* MOLIPO). Most of the ALN's frontline militants, more than 50 of them, were killed between 1969 and 1974. After that, only a handful of ALN militants who were not killed or imprisoned survived the government crackdown.

Brazilian Anti-communist Alliance (*Aliança Anticomunista Brasileira*, AAB)

The AAB was a Brazilian far-right subversive organisation that operated during the military regimes in Brazil and was responsible for several bomb attacks. The group was known for the explosions at the Brazilian Press Association in Rio de Janeiro, on 19 August 1976, which destroyed two bathrooms near the President's office but caused no injuries. Later the same day, another bomb was found in a fuse box at the headquarters of the Brazilian Bar Association (OAB) in Rio de Janeiro, an incident which again caused no casualties. On 9 September, the AAB continued its string of attacks, this time against the Brazilian Centre for Analysis and Planning (*Centro Brasileiro de Análise e Planejamento*, CEBRAP), a research institute in social sciences. On 22 September, Bishop Dom Adriano Hipólito was kidnapped near his home in Nova Iguaçu, beaten, his body painted red, abandoned naked and in the Jacarepaguá suburb of Rio de Janeiro. His car was then taken to the CNBB in Glória and destroyed in an explosion. That same morning, the president of *Organizações Globo*, Roberto Marinho, was also the victim of an attack, a bomb exploding on the roof of his residence in Cosme Velho, a suburb of Rio de Janeiro, destroying part of the second floor. The group also gained notoriety by using explosives to attack the house of businessman and journalist Roberto Marinho. Their *modus operandi* was similar to that of Argentina's infamous Triple A organisation.

In the early 1960s, the first anti-communist civic-military groups emerged in Brazil, adopting violent tactics, the main ones being the MAC and the CCC. These groups carried out, even under the government of João Goulart, acts of terrorism that continued until the early 1970s. The focus of these groups was initially to stop the advance of the Left in Brazil during the Cold War, as the fear of communism was widespread. These groups took part in intense activity from 1961–1964 to prevent communist militants from emulating the achievements of the Cuban Revolution and other recent conflicts.

After the 1964 *coup d'état*, attention focused on the formation of 'security communities', where civilians and members of the military from official intelligence and repression agencies divided into various paramilitary groups (including some members of the AAB) to identify, persecute and torture opponents of the regime. These anti-communist groups had links with the intelligence agencies of the armed forces of Brazil; their actions were never investigated and there are no records of them. The government did not carry out any action to dismantle these organisations, with the SNI trying to hide all evidence related to the AAB.

The AAB claimed to be behind some of the attacks carried out, but the authorities did not identify anyone as being responsible. On 23 September, an entire schedule of the TV newscast *Jornal Nacional* was censored, which was to have been dedicated to investigating kidnappings and bomb attacks. The group also called for an attack on the headquarters of the independent newspaper *Opinión*, carried

On the left, the headquarters of the UNE was attacked by the MAC with bullets and stones, right-wing activists painting the words 'House of the lackeys of Moscow'. On the right, another MAC slogan: 'Let's shoot the Communists'. (Open source)

A poster with photos of members of the CCC containing the warning: 'CCC, the terror commando. They are proud to belong to an organisation that supports extreme right-wing terror. There are many of them and the organisation is large. They are all violent and some are even cowards'. (*O Cruzeiro* magazine)

out on 15 November. Later in December, the headquarters of *Editora Civilização Brasileira* was also attacked by the group, causing serious damage. After these attacks, the group became largely inactive.

Marxist Revolutionary Workers Political Organisation (*Organização Revolucionária Marxista Política Operária*, POLOP)

Long before 1964, POLOP advocated the path of armed revolution, which was to be carried out under the leadership of the working class. During the first half of 1964, POLOP leaders in Rio de Janeiro tried to start a rural guerrilla together with former members of the military in the state of Minas Geráis, which would be called the *Guerrilha de Copacabana*, but the project was thwarted when it was infiltrated by elements of naval intelligence. The young members of the organisation instead formed other groups such as the Communist Workers Party (*Partido Operário Comunista*, POC) and the National Liberation Command (*Comando de Libertação Nacional*, COLINA) in order to be able to launch direct action against the state.

Trotskyist Revolutionary Workers' Party (*Partido Operário Revolucionario Trotskysta*, PORT)

This was a Trotskyist political party that had its roots in the unions but did not have many adherents. It slowly became extinct, its leadership only being interested in political theory, which was why it never attracted the youth among its ranks.

National Liberation Command (*Comando de Libertação Nacional*, COLINA)

The National Liberation Command, also simply known as 'Commandos' in Brazil, was an armed organisation of the extreme Brazilian Left that sought to install a communist regime in the country, similar to that of revolutionary Cuba after its radicalisation in 1961. It intended to fight against the military *de facto* governments from 1964 onwards. COLINA operated primarily during the 1960s, espousing ideas of a leftist insurrectional revolution advocated by the Organization of Solidarity of the Peoples of Africa, Asia and Latin America (*Organización de Solidaridad de los Pueblos de África, Asia y América Latina*, OSPAAL), beginning armed actions in 1968, not only as a form of propaganda but as a way of seeking finance for an eventual rural guerrilla war. The group originated in 1967 in the state of Minas Geráis, through the merger of POLOP with some leftist members of the military, embracing the ideas of OLAS and OSPAAL, and carrying out armed rural guerrilla actions from 1968.

COLINA's leadership had received information that Bolivian Army Captain Gary Prado Salmón was in Brazil studying at the Brazilian Army Command and General Staff School. Prado had become famous as the officer who captured the Marxist revolutionary Che Guevara on 8 October 1967 near La Higuera in Bolivia. COLINA decided to avenge Che's subsequent death, planning to assassinate Prado. On 1 July 1968, João Lucas Alves, Severino Viana Colon, José Roberto Monteiro and Amílcar Baiardi killed a military officer in the Rio neighbourhood of Gávea, believing that he was the Bolivian Prado, when in reality he was West German Army Major Edward Ernest Tito Otto Maximilian

West German Army Major Edward Ernest Tito Otto Maximilian von Westernhagen, a Second World War veteran, was killed by COLINA (left). Two of the murderers of the German officer, former FAB Sergeant João Lucas Alves (centre) and Severino Viana Colon (left). (Open source)

From subversive to President of the Republic. Dilma Rousseff, a member of COLINA in the early 1970s. On the left, being tried in a military court. She is also shown as a DOPS prisoner (centre). Rousseff would go on to become President of Brazil in 2010 (right). (Open source)

von Westernhagen. Realising the fatal misunderstanding, COLINA did not assume responsibility for the attack.

In November 1968, João Lucas was arrested, tortured and killed. Three months later, Severino was captured and imprisoned, later being found dead in his cell after allegedly committing suicide. Homicides disguised as suicide were a relatively common practice at this time, as the death of journalist Vladimir Herzog would later reveal.

In January 1969, the Civil Police of the state of Minas Geráis were involved in a shootout with militants of the COLINA organisation while they were searching for one of its cells, resulting in the death of two police officers. State forces eventually managed to dismantle the group and capture its main leaders. One of these leaders, Murilo Pezzuti, was used as a guinea pig in novel types of torture to obtain information about his guerrilla comrades. In the same year, when several COLINA militants were imprisoned, the organisation morphed into the Palmares Revolutionary Armed Vanguard (*Vanguarda Armada Revolucionaria-Palmares*, VAR-Palmares), after its merger with former members of the VPR (see below).

The most famous member of COLINA was Dilma Rousseff, who was elected President of Brazil in the second round of elections held on 31 October 2010. There were other instances in Latin American countries where former guerrillas became national leaders through democratic elections: José Mujica (a former member of the Tupamaro urban guerrilla) in Uruguay, Salvador Sánchez Cerén (a former FMLM guerrilla) in El Salvador and Gustavo Petro (a former M-19 guerrilla) in Colombia, just to cite some of the most well-known. Other former guerrillas simply became dictators without ever being elected, such as the Sandinista insurgent Daniel Ortega in Nicaragua, and Fidel and Raúl Castro in Cuba. Although Rousseff joined the COLINA organisation in her youth, she had only secondary or peripheral involvement in it actions.

Leonel Brizola, founder of the Groups of Eleven/Gr11. (Open source).

Groups of Eleven (*Grupos dos Onze*, Gr11)

The *Grupos de Onze Companheiros* (Groups of Eleven Companions), shortened as *Grupos dos Onze* or even the Nationalist Commandos, was an urban and rural guerrilla movement conceived at the end of 1963. It was inspired by the formation of a soccer team (with 11 players), an image of easy assimilation and popular appeal. The leader of the group was Leonel Brizola, who organised it in small cells, each of them composed of 11 men, throughout the national territory that could be mobilised under his command. It was a left-wing group, not communist but nationalist, and openly supported the basic policies of some nationalist politicians, in the context of radicalisation during the military regimes. Brizola did not sympathise at all with Brazil's communist leaders, whom he accused of being bourgeois under the orders of Moscow with a completely distorted vision of reality.

From 1962, Brizola aired a program every Friday at 9:00 p.m. on the *Mairink Veiga* radio station. Through his radio proclamations, Brizola's voice reached the most distant parts of Brazil, mobilising the population around his political ideas and proposals to change

The PCdoB flag of a red field with the communist emblem and letters in yellow (left). The three main leaders of the Araguaia Guerrilla, from left to right, Maurício Grabois, Pedro Pomar and João Amazonas (right). (Open source)

the country. On the night of 29 November 1963, Brizola launched the movement known as Gr11.

Brizola had been a federal deputy elected in 1962 for the former state of Guanabara and was leader of the Popular Mobilisation Front (a group of organisations and sectors of various parties pushing for basic reforms). With the formation of the Gr11 groups, Brizola intended to have an organised and popular extra-parliamentary force. The organisation of the Nationalist Commandos was directly related to the climate of insecurity that surrounded the government of João Goulart.

When the Gr11s were created, radicalisation had already become widespread in Brazil. The main objectives of these 'commandos' were organised action in defence of the democratic conquests of common people, the institution of an authentic and nationalist democracy, the immediate realisation of reforms – especially agrarian and urban reforms – and a sacred determination to fight for the liberation of their homeland from international plunder. Brizola's followers were known as *Brizolistas*.

At the beginning of 1964, Brizola launched his own weekly newspaper, *O Panfleto* (*The Pamphlet*), which became part of the campaign already developed by the *Mairink Veiga* radio station. A total of 5,304 groups were organised, comprising 58,344 people, distributed, in particular, throughout the states of Rio Grande do Sul, Guanabara, Rio de Janeiro, Minas Geráis and São Paulo. Those groups were mainly formed from friends and neighbours who carefully read the instructions and manuals given by their leaders. Each group elected a leader, an assistant and a secretary/treasurer. There were two members in each group in charge of communications, and the rest of the members were in charge of listening to the news on the radio, transport, propaganda, popular mobilisation, information and medical and social assistance. Each group could contact the national leadership through a liaison officer. Although there were no restrictions to becoming a member, the Gr11s practically ignored the militant women. The Gr11s were suffocated and aborted from their origin by the coup of 1964 and Brizola's exile in Uruguay during the military regimes. Some remnants of the Gr11s continued their political militancy within legal institutions.

Araguaia Guerrilla (*Guerrilha do Araguaia*)

As an immediate precedent, the PCdoB had split from the PCB in February 1962, these dissidents being of the orthodox pro-China line. Its main leaders were Maurício Grabois, Pedro Pomar and João Amazonas. They also advocated armed struggle against the military regime through a rural guerrilla, creating what was later called the *Araguaia Guerrilla*.

The *Araguaia Guerrilla* was a subversive movement that existed in the Brazilian Amazon region, along the Araguaia River, between the late 1960s and the mid-1970s. Its objective was to foster a socialist revolution, to be initiated in the countryside, based on the successful experiences of the Cuban and Chinese Revolutions.

The Brazilian armed forces entered into combat with this guerrilla movement in 1972, when several of the organisation's members had already established themselves in the region for at least six years. The stage for combat operations between the guerrillas and the military was in the states of Goiás, Pará and Maranhão, close to the cities of São Geraldo do Araguaia and Marabá in Pará and Xambioá in the north of Goiás.

It is estimated that the movement was made up of 85 guerrillas, of which 17 survived, including the former president of the Workers' Party (PT), José Genoíno, who was detained by the Brazilian Army in 1972 in the first phase of military operations. The majority of combatants, made up mainly of former university students and professionals, were killed in jungle combat or executed after their capture by the military during the final operations between 1973 and 1974. More than 60 of them are still today considered to be among the politically 'disappeared'.

Unknown to the rest of the country at the time it occurred, protected by a curtain of silence and censorship to which the movement and the military operations against it were subjected, details about the guerrilla movement only began to appear around 20 years after Brazil returned with democratic elected governments. More details of this guerrilla and the Brazilian armed forces operations against it are covered in the corresponding chapters in this volume.

8 October Revolutionary Movement (*Movimento Revolucionário 8 de* Outubro, MR-8)

The MR-8 was a left-wing organisation with a Marxist-Leninist ideology, which fought against the Brazilian military regimes. Its objective was the establishment of a state on the Soviet model. The date 8 October was chosen for its name because that was when Ernesto Che Guevara was captured by Bolivian Army Rangers in 1967. Guevara, a symbolic figure since his death later that year, was the inspiration for a wave of guerrilla movements around the world in the 1960s and 1970s. MR-8 was formed in 1966 and was originally known as *Dissidência da Guanabara* (Guanabara Dissidence). Their actions occurred at the local university in that state. It gained worldwide fame when guerrillas from the group kidnapped American Ambassador Charles Burke Elbrick in a joint attack with *Ação Libertadora Nacional* on 4 September 1969.

As a result of a split with the PCB, the MR-8 participated in several actions of the student movement and the beginning of the armed

The MR-8 flag, in green and yellow with red letters and emblem (left). Two prominent members of the MR-8, Tara Tavelberg and Carlos Lamarca, a former Brazilian Army captain (right). (Open source)

struggle in 1968. Dismantled by the Brazilian Army in early 1969, its survivors joined members of the Guanabara Communist Dissidence (DI-GB) in political demonstrations under the leadership of Vladimir Palmeira, and together they reconstituted a 'new' MR-8.

MR-8 fought in a similar way to other urban guerrillas in Brazil and elsewhere around South America, such as the *Montoneros* in Argentina or the *Tupamaros* in Uruguay, carrying out assaults against banks and businesses, especially in the Rio de Janeiro area. In 1971, MR-8 expressed its support for the defection of Army Captain Carlos Lamarca to the ranks of the Popular Revolutionary Vanguard (*Vanguarda Popular Revolucionária*, VPR), another guerrilla group. Lamarca later enlisted in MR-8 when the VPR was eradicated by the military regime in 1970 and fought with the group until his death on 17 September 1971 in an ambush in Pintada, a town in the state of Bahía. Another famous guerrilla member of the MR-8 organisation was Iara Iavelberg, Captain Lamarca's mistress, who was murdered just two days after him in strange circumstances. Lamarca's death was widely publicised by the government through the media in order to show the fate of anyone who became involved in terrorist activities. According to the National Truth Commission, which later investigated human rights violations in the country, 434 opponents of the military regime in Brazil died or disappeared between 1946 and 1988, the majority of them during the *de facto* governments from 1964–1985.

Around 1972, MR-8 sent most of its militants to Chile, where they joined the Chilean Revolutionary Left Movement (*Movimiento de Izquierda Revolucionaria*, MIR). In the following phases of the Brazilian military regimes, MR-8 focused primarily on infiltrating the legal opposition in Brazil, especially the Brazilian Democratic Movement. The MR-8 newspaper was *Hora do Povo* (*People's Hour*), which is still published to this day. In addition to Gabeira and Lamarca, other militants who formed MR-8 included the journalists and politicians Franklin Martins and César Benjamin. MR-8 did not dissolve over time, and continues to maintain a presence in the PMDB, the trade union the General Confederation of Brazilian Workers (*Confederação Geral dos Trabalhadores*, CGTB) and among university students. It also has a youth arm, the 8 October Revolutionary Youth (*Juventude Revolucionária Oito de Outubro*, JR-8).

Brazilian Revolutionary Communist Party (*Partido Comunista Brasileiro Revolucionário*, PCBR)

The PCBR was a leftist political party in Brazil, founded in 1968 by Mário Alves, Jacob Gorender and Apolônio de Carvalho from the PCB. The origins of the PCBR dated back to 1964, when its then main leader, Mário Alves, a journalist and intellectual within the executive branch of the PCB, began to oppose the positions held by Luís Carlos Prestes in the Central Committee of the party, forming the so-called Revolutionary Current (*Corrente Revolucionária*) with some strength in Rio de Janeiro and the northeast of Brazil. After their proposals had been defeated at the Sixth Congress of the PCB, partly due to bureaucratic manoeuvres by the party leadership, that prevented the participation of the main delegates of the Revolutionary Current in April 1968, the dissidents decided to found the PCBR in Rio de Janeiro. The PCBR proposed the constitution of a new Marxist party that reformulated the traditional line of the PCB regarding the need for an alliance with the Brazilian bourgeoisie, without embracing the idea of an immediate socialist revolution.

In terms of its strategy, the peculiarity of the PCBR was its combination of the rural guerrilla and work to raise awareness of the masses in the cities, with a view to the formation of an eventual 'revolutionary popular government'. This government would supposedly carry out 'democratic and anti-imperialist' tasks, which would open the way to the socialist revolution, in a formulation that was close to the Trotskyist formula of permanent revolution.

From April 1969, the PCBR was busy carrying out armed urban guerrilla operations, essentially oriented towards propaganda. The intensification of repression in the second half of that year forced the party to launch more daring operations. After the first robbery of a bank carried out by the PCBR in Rio de Janeiro, a series of imprisonments began that included members of the Central Committee of the party, with hundreds of the group's militants jailed by the Brazilian military regime. According to a survey carried out by the Brazil: Never Again (*Brasil: Nunca Mais*) movement, 31 judicial cases related to the PCBR took place, with some 400 citizens captured and accused during investigations or background checks. At least 16 militants were killed or disappeared due to military repression.

The PCBR had bases in Guanabara, the state of Rio de Janeiro and a smaller one in São Paulo. In the northeast, in the states of Bahía and Ceará, they had a support base much superior to any dissident faction of the PCB and capable of competing in the leftist media. In the state of Paraná, the PCBR expanded in the city of Londrina.

In January 1970, the repression unleashed by the military government hit the party hard, including the imprisonment of Salatiel Teixeira Rolim. After having been tortured, Salatiel revealed the location of various clandestine shelters of the PCBR. By 12 January, Apolônio de Carvalho, Mário Alves, Miguel Batista, Jacob Gorender, Renê Carvalho, Álvaro Caldas and several other leaders had been captured and sent to prison, which caused the demise of the PCBR. In mid-1973, after being released from prison, Teixeira Rolim was

A PCR poster showing a map of Brazil and the main leaders of the left. The phrase at the top says 'Down with the Dictatorship'. (Open source)

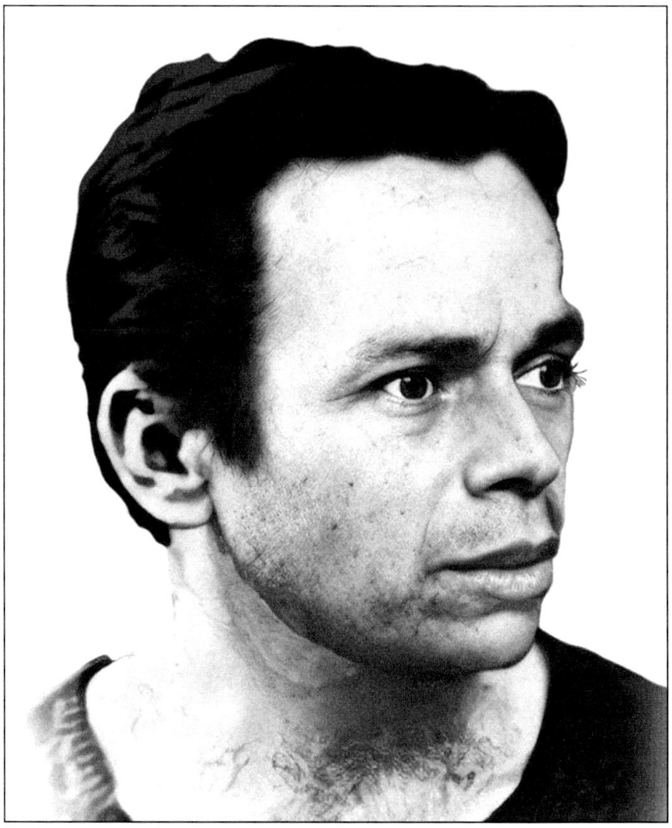

PCR leader Amaro Luiz de Carvalho. (Open source)

shot dead in the bar where he worked by a commando of three PCBR militants, who accused him of being a traitor, an act that was condemned by many militants, both inside and outside the organisation. In the late 1970s, some surviving remnants of the party participated in the founding of the Workers' Party (PT).

Revolutionary Communist Party (*Partido Comunista Revolucionário*, PCR)

The PCR was a Hoxhaist communist political party in Brazil. It was inspired by the ideas proposed by the Albanian politician and military dictator Enver Halil Hoxha, who led the People's Socialist Republic of Albania from 1944 until his death in 1985. It emerged as a splinter group from the PCdoB in May 1966 in Recife, where it was founded.

The PCR was organised by a group of militants who had left the PCdoB and were dissatisfied with the Maoist direction it was taking, criticising it as being inflexible. From the beginning, the PCR faced a fierce struggle against what they described as the 'deviations' of Leninism in the international communist movement.

After the 1964 coup, and despite the danger it consequently faced, the PCR remained committed to the armed struggle against the military government. The party was instrumental in organising labour strikes and student demonstrations, but also engaged in more destructive activities such as burning government-owned sugar cane fields. The party was partially dismantled in the early 1970s after the government launched a brutal torture campaign against suspected communists and left-wing political parties. The party's leader, Amaro Luiz de Carvalho, was arrested and later killed by the police. Other prominent members of the party were murdered, and on 12 May 1978, Carvalho's successor, Edival Nunes Cajá, was captured. In response, more than 12,000 students from the Federal University of Pernambuco went on strike in Recife, where Cajá was being held. The student protest eventually secured his release, although he was arrested again soon after for publicly detailing the torture he had suffered while in prison. He would not be permanently released until 1 June 1979. In July 1981, due to the limited success of the PCR's resistance operations against the government, the party made the decision to merge with MR-8, an urban guerrilla organisation that had also separated from the PCdoB years before.

MR-8 also publicly declared itself Marxist-Leninist, but its bourgeois organisational structure and affinity with 'bourgeois nationalism' led to serious disagreements with former PCR members. After internal struggles, the PCR chose to split from MR-8 in 1985, resulting in the re-founding of the party. This new version of the political party survives to this day.

Communist Workers Party (*Partido Operário Comunista*, POC)

The POC was a left-wing Brazilian organisation that fought against the military *de facto* regimes established in Brazil in 1964, in an attempt to create a socialist government in the country. It was founded in 1968 from another organisation, POLOP.

When the POC decided to move towards armed struggle, some of its militants created the Workers' Political Marxist Revolutionary Organisation (OCML-PO), also known as Nova POLOP. The POC maintained a certain presence within the student movement of 1968, where it was known as the Critical University Movement (*Movimento Universidade Crítica*), in addition to having some participation among the working class in the Brazilian state capitals.

In April 1970, a group of militants broke away from the POC to re-establish POLOP. For their part, those who remained in the group began to have deep internal disagreements, some of its members defending joint action with various Brazilian urban guerrilla groups of the time, such as *Acción Libertadora Nacional*, *Vanguardia Popular Revolucionaria* and VAR-Palmares, even participating in several armed operations.

By 1971, however, the group had been practically dismantled by the Brazilian military regime, despite eventually carrying out sporadic insurgent acts from abroad. Among the POC militants killed as a result of the repression carried out by the military government were Luiz Eduardo da Rocha Merlino, Hélio Zanir Sanchotene Trindade and Ary Abreu Lima. POC members Luiz Carlos Almeida and Nelson Kohl were killed in Chile during the military coup that overthrew the Marxist President Salvador Allende on 11 September 1973.

Nationalist Armed Resistance (*Resistência Armada Nacionalista*, RAN)

The RAN was a Brazilian guerrilla group under the leadership of former Admiral Cândido de Assis da Costa Aragão, who brought together former Army and Air Force officers and NCOs. According to CIA data, the group had an escape network and a guerrilla support base in Bolivia, where contacts, names and addresses were found in Porto Alegre. Concentrated in Montevideo, it was dominated by members of the military exiled by the regime.

Originally founded as the Nationalist Military Resistance Movement (*Movimento de Resistência Militar Nacionalista*, MRMN), around December 1966 it became the Nationalist Armed Resistance (*Resistencia Armada Nacionalista*, RAN), using as its emblem a frog like Paraíba's marines in the Brazilian Navy. The RAN planned to obtain economic resources from the Communist Party of Uruguay (PCU) and OLAS, through contacts with Rodney Arismendi and Edmundo Soares Neto. They launched a subversive manifesto signed by Cândido Aragão, especially aimed at the capitals of the states of Rio Grande do Sul, São Paulo, Guanabara and Rio de Janeiro. Later, the plan was to send groups to Cuba and North Korea to be trained in guerrilla warfare.

In March 1966, RAN leaders met with Leonel Brizola of the Gr11s for proposed joint actions, but they could not reach an agreement so the groups went their separate ways. Above all, the former military personnel were reluctant to accept Brizola's leadership, as a result of the repeated failures of his previous attempts, which they classified as irresponsible adventures.

On 20 May 1966, a meeting of the military group was held at the residence of former Admiral Cândido da Costa Aragão, in Montevideo, in order to establish an organisation that could operate clandestinely in Brazil. At that meeting, it was established that the MRMN would initially unleash a series of acts against targets linked to US interests in Brazil. In a later phase, it would push for the physical elimination of members of the Peace Corps and other Americans who were supposedly CIA agents. The MRMN believed that these acts would provoke violent repression which, in turn, would lead to the climate that the organisation aimed for, which it called 'self-defence of the masses'. From there, the MRMN, gaining more followers, would lead an armed revolution by a well-constituted guerrilla movement.

Initially, the head of the MRMN was former Admiral Aragão. Later, due to health problems, he handed over command to Alfredo Ribeiro Daudt and Emanoel Nicoll. The MRMN included ex-military exiles in Uruguay and other countries, ex-military members disbanded in Brazil and, clandestinely, some military personnel still in active service, recruited under the banner of nationalism, an omnipresent thought for the majority of military personnel. To do this, the bases of the movement would be moved to Rio Grande do Sul, with the intention of recruiting military personnel and civilians, who would participate in the organisation by forming 'nuclei of resistance' in several cities in Brazil.

On 26 May 1966, the MRMN published the manifesto *Ao Povo Brasileiro* (*To the Brazilian People*), in which it conveyed a hegemonic image of Brazil in South America. At the beginning of June, the MRMN tried unsuccessfully to approach the union group of the exiles. The unionists believed that the activity of the ex-military personnel negatively affected the work that Dante Pelacani was doing in São Paulo, in relation to Benedito Cerqueira and with the World Federation of Trade Unions. That same day in June 1966, the MRMN contacted the Cuba Support Committee to obtain its political recognition.

On 15 June, former president João Goulart (also known as *Jango*) organised, at his residence, a meeting with the MRMN, represented by Aragão, Daudt and Nicoll, in which Darcy Ribeiro and Amaury Silva also participated. *Jango* promised economic aid to the movement and, trying to stay above the groups, created a committee to coordinate them, made up of Emanoel Nicoll, representing the military group, Dante Pelacani (for the union), Neiva Moreira (the *Brizolistas*) and Darcy Ribeiro, representing *Jango* himself. This hodgepodge of leaders with different visions of what would have to be done to overthrow the *de facto* military regime did not reach any agreement, each one following their own path, something very common in left-wing political movements and parties, with too many leaders and not enough members.

Determined to emerge from political anonymity and seek economic support, the MRMN came out of inactivity, carrying out an attack on 21 October 1966 with explosives against the monument to the Baron of Rio Branco in Montevideo, executed by Gualter de Castro Mello, Tito Guimarães Filho and Arnaldo Magno de Araújo. In December 1966, the MRMN leadership decided to change the name of the organisation to the RAN. The new RAN struggled to impose itself and be recognised, its attempts frustrated by the ruling military regime.

National Liberation Armed Forces (*Forças Armadas de Libertação Nacional*, FALN)

The National Liberation Armed Forces (FALN) was an organisation that operated very briefly from 1967 until 1969. The movement was created in Ribeirão Preto, first being called the National Liberation Front before later being renamed the National Liberation Armed Forces. The FALN was structured into three well-defined sectors: intelligence, logistics and training of personnel. The idea was to form a Popular Liberation Army to overthrow the military regime.

The FALN was a dissenting group from the Municipal Committee of the PCB in the city of Ribeirão Preto, a process that began in 1966, when a group of students would also end up opting for armed struggle but would not join existing groups. The organisation spread across 40 municipalities in the region, counting among its members students, intellectuals, workers and peasants, as well as religious people. It was dismantled in mid-October 1969 following the arrest of their effectives in a camp near the city of Sertãozinho. Most served prison sentences ranging from two-and-a-half to five years. Vanderley Caixe served five years after being identified as the group's coordinator. Mario Bugliani (known as *The Captain*), a peasant, served four years and Aurea Moretti three years.

Its informative organ, the newspaper *O Berro* (*The Scream*), was not created by the organisation. It was, however, appropriated by the FALN at some point, as it already existed before the group that would give rise to the FALN. The content of *O Berro* was not aimed at a specific social segment. Despite its large circulation among rural workers, the intention was to disseminate it to as many social segments as possible. In 1968, shaken by the eruption of the student movement on a global scale, the FALN identified itself with Debrayism (ideas disseminated by Régis Debray), with its theory of the guerrilla focus. Due to the displacement of its staff to the sugarcane area, *O Berro* stopped aiming its content at students and leaned towards rural workers. After the

The VAR-Palmares emblem. Some leaders of this organisation, from left to right: former Army captain Carlos Lamarca, Carlos Alberto Soares de Freitas, Mariano Joaquim da Silva and Carlos Franklin Paixão de Araújo. (Open source)

enacting of Institutional Act Nr.5, the FALN accelerated the process of preparing for guerrilla warfare, the organisation having already carried out tactical training in the countryside. After a FALN assault on a quarry to steal dynamite, a militant was located in the forest when he was planning a kidnapping operation.

In the second half of 1967, the FALN began its terrorist attacks in the cities of Ribeirão Preto and Sertãozinho. In the first city, they detonated bombs in several places, including movie theatres, the market, post office, Mormon church and headquarters of the 3rd Battalion of the Military Police. In Sertãozinho, bombs exploded in several public places. These were not of great power so practically no one was injured, but the intention was to effect morale. The FALN left pamphlets expressing their intention to overthrow the government and praising Che Guevara.

The infamous police torturer Sérgio Paranhos Fleury went with his group to the region and more than 500 people were detained there, including some religious people, nuns and priests. Among the prisoners, one case deserves to be highlighted: the arrest of Mother Maurina Borges, a nun, who was savagely tortured. She would only be released in 1970, in exchange for the rescue of the Japanese consul, Nobuo Okuchi, in São Paulo. This kidnapping was organised by the VPR and REDE (Democratic Resistance), although it is possible that the MRT also participated in the operation. By then, the students' attempt, as well as that of several rural workers from Ribeirão Preto, to actively participate in the armed struggle had already come to an end.

Revolutionary Armed Vanguard-Palmares (*Vanguarda Armada Revolucionaria-Palmares*, VAR-Palmares)

VAR-Palmares was a left-wing guerrilla organisation with a Marxist-Leninist ideology founded in 1969, which operated until 1972 in Brazil. Among its leaders were the former Army Captain Carlos Lamarca, Carlos Alberto Soares de Freitas, Mariano Joaquim da Silva and Carlos Franklin Paixão de Araújo. Among the Brazilian politicians who made up the VAR-Palmares were Dilma Rousseff, who was elected President of Brazil in 2010, and Carlos Minc, who in the 1980s would become a pro-ecology activist, founding the Green Party of Brazil. It was created as a consequence of the merger of two previous guerrilla organisations, COLINA and the VPR, which in turn were offshoots of POLOP.

VAR-Palmares was one of the main guerrilla organisations that fought against the military regimes that took power with the *coup d'état* of 1964. Among the most notable actions of VAR-Palmares was the robbery of Adhemar Pereira de Barros's coffers on 18 July 1969, when they stole $2.5 million kept in the house of Anna Gimel Benchimol Capriglione, secretary and lover of Adhemar de Barros, then governor of São Paulo. The money kept in the safe was believed to be the product of the corruption of the former governor. Among others, in addition to commander Juares de Brito and leader Antonio Espinosa, *Sônia* Lafoz was the only important guerrilla in the armed struggle, a participant in bank robberies and kidnappings of diplomats. She was famous for being an expert sniper, and she participated in the action described above. Other guerrillas, who were never arrested, were Darcy Rodrigues, a former soldier and right-hand man of Lamarca, Reinaldo José de Mello, Wellington Moreira Diniz, former Army sergeant José de Araújo Nóbrega, João Marques de Aguiar, former guerrilla butcher João Domingues, Fernando Borges and Jesus Paredes Soto. Carlos Minc, now a politician linked to environmentalism, was one of the members of VAR-Palmares who participated in the assault (he was 18 years old at the time). Dilma Rousseff also participated in the organisation, but she was not involved in the group's best-known action.

In 1969, members of VAR-Palmares planned the kidnapping of Finance Minister Antônio Delfim Netto, planner of the Brazilian Economic Miracle and the most powerful civilian in the regime at the time. The attempted kidnapping took place in December of that year but was unsuccessful because most of the group's members hd been captured and imprisoned a few weeks earlier.

Maurício Lopes Lima, who worked with the intelligence service of the armed forces and was also in charge of torture centres for political prisoners, believed that Dilma Rousseff was the 'brains' of the clandestine organisation, a fact that could never be proven. Antonio Espinosa was, however, a participant in the attempted kidnapping of Delfim Netto and one of the commanders of VAR-Palmares.

After the attack on Delfim Netto, Carlos Lamarca, one of the organisation's commanders, issued the following statement on behalf of VAR-Palmares to a French press agency: 'After a long investigation, we located a part of the famous 'box' of the former governor of São Paulo Adhemar de Barros, enriched by years and years of corruption. We obtained US$ 2.5 million. This money, stolen from the people, will be returned.'[1]

Another prominent VAR-Palmares action was the hijacking of Flight 114 of the airline *Cruzeiro do Sul* on 1 January 1970. The Sud Aviation SE-210 Caravelle VI-R jet, registration PP-PDZ, carried 23 passengers and seven crew members, comprising Mário Amaral (Captain), Silvio Eduardo de Carvalho Fróes (First Officer), Hélio Batista Borges (Flight Engineer), Nerli Baradel (Purser) and José Omar da Silveira Morais, Ogler Passos Soares and Eliete Dias de Carvalho (flight attendants).

The flight started in Montevideo, Uruguay, bound for Rio de Janeiro, with stops in Porto Alegre and São Paulo. Once the Caravelle

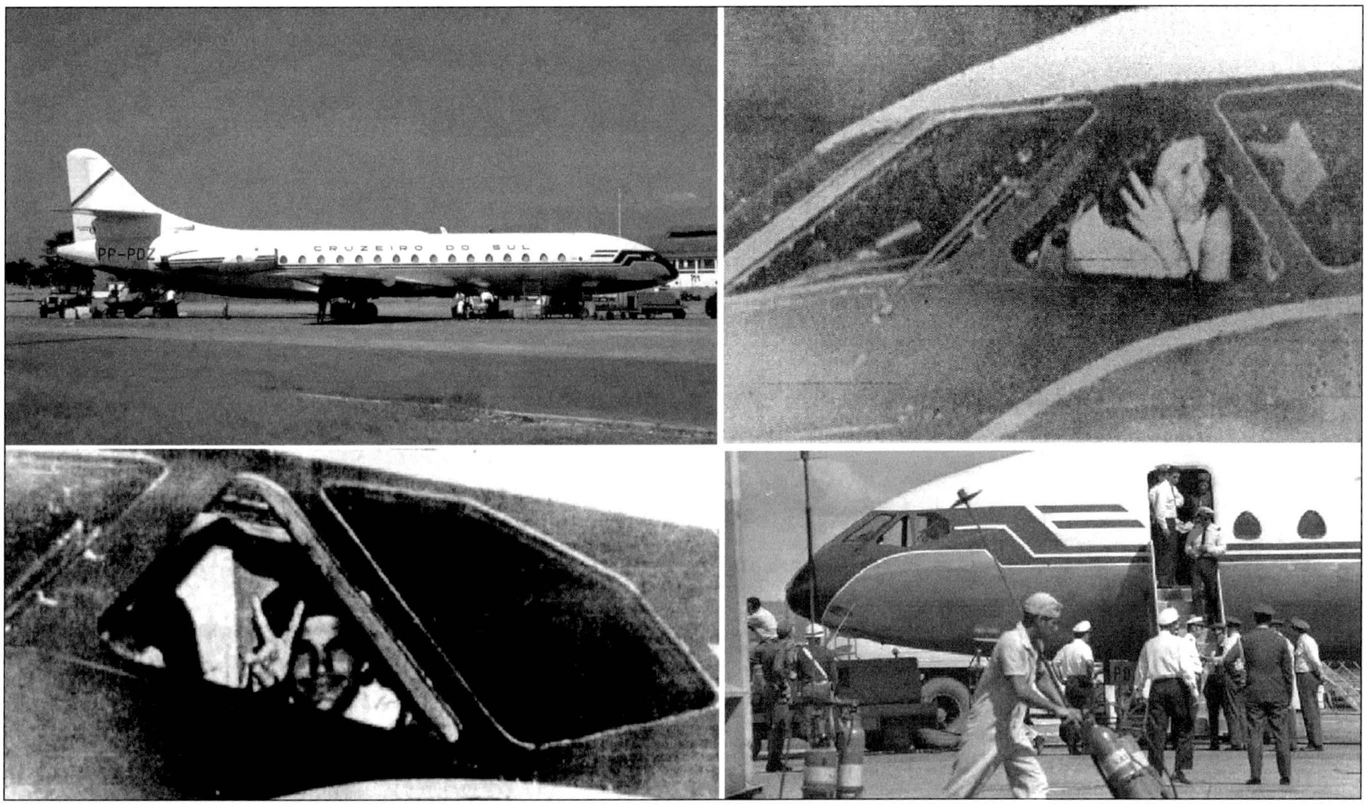

Above left, the *Cruzeiro do Sul* airlines Sud Aviation SE-210 Caravelle VI-R registration PP-PDZ. Hijacker Marília Guimarães peeking out of the flight deck (top right). Another of the hijackers in the cabin of the aircraft (below left) and the aircraft in Brazil after a long and tiresome flight (below right). (Hélio Bastos Salmon; *O Globo* archives)

took off, the five hijackers took control of the aircraft. The hijackers were Cláudio Galeno de Magalhães Linhares (Dilma Rousseff's first husband), James Allen da Luz, Athos Magno Costa e Silva, Isolde Sommer and Marília Guimarães (with her two sons, who at that time were aged two and three). The hijackers forced the pilot to fly first to Buenos Aires, then to Antofagasta in Chile and Lima, Peru, where they spent 27 hours due to a technical problem with a battery. Once the issue was solved, the aircraft departed for Havana, Cuba, where it arrived on 3 January after a stop in Panama City. The hijackers stayed in Cuba as political refugees, and the Caravelle and all its passengers and crew members finally returned to Rio de Janeiro – after stops in Puerto Rico, Manáus and Brasília – on 7 January.

VAR-Palmares was officially dismantled in 1972 due to strong repression by the military, some of its main leaders having been imprisoned and murdered by the regime.

Popular Revolutionary Vanguard (*Vanguarda Popular Revolucionária*, VPR)

The VPR was a Brazilian Marxist-Leninist guerrilla organisation that fought against the military regimes with the aim of establishing a socialist republic in the country. It was formed in 1966 from a dissident faction of POLOP and some military remnants of the MNR.

On 25 January 1969, Army Captain Carlos Lamarca decided to join the guerrilla movement. He stole an Army VW Kombi van from the Quitaúna barracks in Osasco, where he was serving, filled it with 63 assault rifles, 10 machine guns, ammunition and explosives, and then fled.

On 9 May 1969, the group staged one of its first attacks. High-impact actions it carried out included assaults on the Mercantil de São Paolo and Itaú banks, which left a bank guard dead from two shots to the head. Both robberies were successful and the VPR was able to raise funds to keep the wing armed. On 11 March 1970, the Japanese Consul General in São Paulo, Nobuo Okushi, was kidnapped. The consul was chased by three vehicles and abducted and held for just one day. He was released in exchange for five political prisoners being released.

On 5 April, the US Consul General in Brazil, Curtis C. Cutter, was injured after an attempted kidnapping in Porto Alegre. According to police, Mr Cutter, his wife Catherine, and a friend, Hovey Clark, were driving home after dinner when a small blue car suddenly drove in front of Cutter's car, forcing the Consul to stop. Witnesses said four or five men armed with submachine guns, wearing dark glasses and lowered hats, jumped out of the small car. Cutter stepped on the accelerator and drove at the armed men, knocking one of them off the hood of his car. The Consul's car then ran over the gunman, who opened fire, slightly injuring Cutter.

The VPR also planned to form a rural guerrilla, choosing Vale do Ribeira, in the state of São Paulo, as a training location. Under the coordination of former Captain Lamarca, several members of the VPR were trained there for five months, but due to confessions under torture from some of their comrades, the Army learned of the existence of the guerrilla training camp.

In April 1970, knowing these plans, the government launched *Operação Registro* (Operation Registry), which consisted of the mobilisation of 1,500 Army troops from the 1st Battalion of the 4th Infantry Regiment, the 2nd Battalion of Hunters (*Caçadores*) and the 6th Motorized Coast Artillery Group. They surrounded the VPR training camp and a bloody fight ensued. The Army was supported by four UH-1H helicopters and five armed T-6Ds from the FAB. The troops surrounded the area and blocked all access roads. Parachute troops from the Airborne Brigade – comprising 11 officers, 17 NCOs and six corporals, carrying dogs trained for military operations – were mobilised to the area in a FAB DHC-5/C-115 Buffalo.

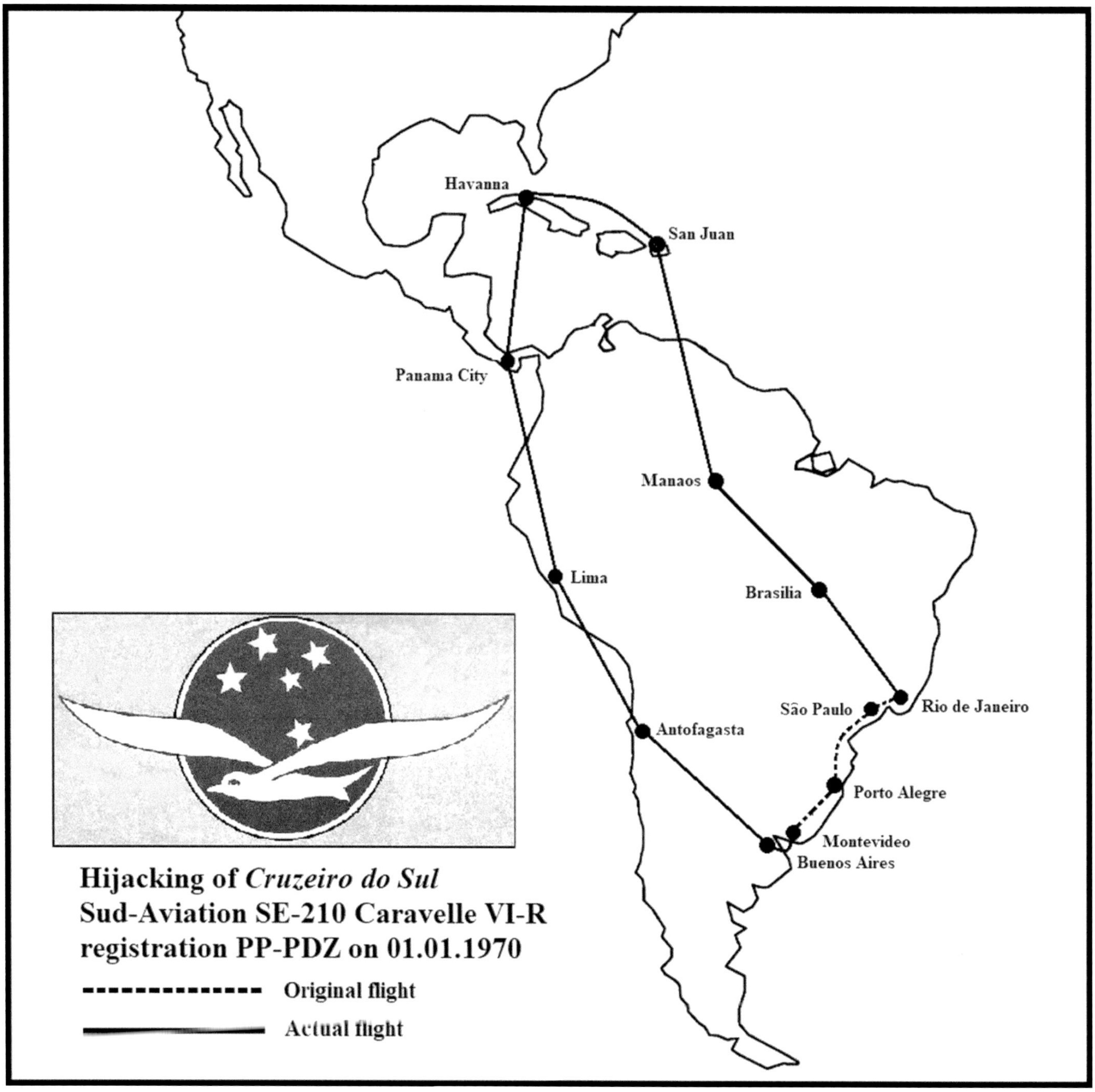

The itinerary of the hijacked *Cruzeiro do Sul* Caravelle PP-PDZ. (Map by author)

Seeing the forcefulness of the military deployment, Lamarca and the VPR members fled north, being pursued by the paratroopers. During their escape, they were machinegunned and bombed by FAB T-6Ds and UH-1s. Many subversives were wounded and captured, but others managed to escape, disguised as civilians, among them Lamarca, Fujimore, Gilberto, Diógenes, Nóbrega, Ariston and Edmauro. Nevertheless, one by one, they were subsequently all killed by the security forces, including Carlos Lamarca himself, on 17 September 1971.

On 29 April 1970, a raid by FAB UH-1 helicopters was carried out in an area where the remnants of the VPR were taking refuge. There were also continuous counterinsurgency operations in the jungle, where government forces confiscated material found in caves, huts and other shelters built by the guerrillas.

On 11 June, Ehrenfried Von Holloben, the West German Ambassador in Brazil, was kidnapped. The kidnapping occurred outside the Ambassador's residence in Santa Teresa. Two police officers who were part of the Ambassador's bodyguard and in an escort vehicle were shot, one of them fatally. Holloben was freed on 16 June after the group demanded that 41 guerrillas be released and sent to Algeria. The kidnappers justified the kidnapping by saying that German companies were involved in the 'exploitation of Brazil'.

On 7 December 1970, Giovanni Enrico Bucher, the Swiss Ambassador to Brazil, was kidnapped by the VPR in the Flamengo neighbourhood, south of Rio de Janeiro, from where he was taken to a house occupied by the kidnappers. During the operation, Hélio Carvalho de Araújo, one of the Federal Police agents who was working with the Ambassador's security team and was inside the Embassy's blue Buick vehicle, was shot dead by the guerrillas. In exchange for the life of the Swiss Ambassador, the VPR demanded that the government release 70 political prisoners. They also demanded a general price freeze in the Brazilian economy for 90 days. At the time, this was

The 70 political prisoners released by the government for the freedom of the kidnapped Swiss Ambassador to Brazil, Giovanni Enrico Bucher. They would then board a VARIG 707 for the flight to exile in Chile (left). The VPR emblem (right). (Open source)

Two foreign diplomats kidnapped by the VPR. The Consul General of Japan in São Paulo, Nobuo Okushi (left), and the Swiss Ambassador to Brazil, Giovanni Enrico Bucher (right). (Open source)

the largest demand made for the release of a kidnapped diplomat. Bucher became the victim of the longest political kidnapping ever to occur in Brazil. The military government, which had quickly given in to the kidnappers' demands in previous cases, this time decided to toughen up and refused to release 13 of the prisoners included on the list sent by the VPR. The stalemate, which lasted for weeks, led to the decision to eliminate Bucher, made by the majority of the kidnappers and the VPR. Nevertheless, the Swiss diplomat was not killed, thanks to the intervention of Lamarca, who, as the group's leader, assumed responsibility for accepting the government's counterproposals, thereby saving Bucher's life. After another month in the hands of the guerrillas, Bucher's sense of humour, kindness and personality had helped him establish a good personal relationship with the guerrillas. Bucher was eventually released on the morning of 16 January 1971, near the Da Penha church in northern Rio de Janeiro, three days after the setting free of 70 prisoners, 13 of whom had replaced those originally requested but were denied by the government. The prisoners were sent into exile in Chile. It was the last major kidnapping during the rule of the military regimes in Brazil.

After this series of attacks, several militants were captured and subjected to torture or extrajudicial executions by the Brazilian security forces. Some of these insurgents fled to countries such as Argentina, Chile and Mexico between September 1969 and March 1970.

After its merger with COLINA, the VAR-Palmares organisation emerged. The VPR was later reorganised, and in 1970 it began to establish a guerrilla training camp in the Ribeira Valley. A second area used for this purpose (the first having been abandoned because it was unsuitable) was discovered by the DOI-CODI following a search operation that mobilised almost 5,000 soldiers. The group had some internal problems, as was usual in all leftist guerrilla organisations.

Navy Corporal José Anselmo de Santos, a DOPS agent infiltrated into the VPR, which led to the capture and death of several subversives. (Open source)

After these continuous blows, the VPR opted for self-dissolution in 1971 following the death of José Raimundo da Costa, the last commander of the organisation. Its location had been revealed by Navy Corporal José Anselmo de Santos, an agent from the DOPS infiltrated within the group, which led to the murder of Soledad Barrett, Pauline Reichstul, Eudaldo Gómez da Silva, Jarbas Pereira Márquez, José Manoel da Silva and Evaldo Luiz Ferreira.

Years later, on 22 October 1976, an attack occurred against a business belonging to a former Brazilian Army general, in which no one suffered any injuries. The authorities suspected VPR involvement, but no group claimed responsibility for the attack.

FAB aircraft involved in Operation Registry against the VPR in April 1970: a Bell UH-1H, North American T-6D Texan and De Havilland Canada DCH-5/C-115 Buffalo. (FAB via Hélio Higuchi)

From left to right, VPR subversives Soledad Barrett, Pauline Reichstul, Eudaldo Gómez da Silva, Jarbas Pereira Márquez, José Manoel da Silva and Evaldo Luiz Ferreira, all captured and executed by law enforcement forces. (Open source)

3
BRAZILIAN ARMED FORCES IN THE 1960S AND 1970S

Brazilian Army (*Exército Brasileiro*, EB)

The Brazilian Army has had a long history of warfare since its creation in 1822 and actively participated in the following conflicts: War of Independence (1821–1824), Confederation of Ecuador (1824), Cisplatine War against Argentina (1825–1828), Revolt of the Malês (1835), Dos Cabanos War (1835–1840), Farroupilha Revolution (1835–1845), Bem-te-vis War (1838–1841), Praieira Revolt (1848–1849), Prata War against Argentina and Uruguay (1851–1852), Uruguayan Civil War (1864–1865), Paraguayan War (1864–1870), Armada Revolt (1893–1894), Federalist Revolution (1893-1895), Canudos War (1896–1897), Acre Revolution against Bolivia (1899–1903), Contestado War (1912–1916), First World War (1917–1918), Tenentista Revolts (1922–1927), Revolution of 1930, Constitutionalist Revolution (1932), Communist Uprising (1935), Second World War (1942–1945), Cold War (1964–1985), Operation Power Pack in the Dominican Republic (1965–1966), Condor Operation (1968–1985) and the Araguaia

TABLE 1: Brazilian Army Ministers 1963–1985

Minister	Dates	
	From	To
Army General Jair Dantas Ribeiro	14 June 1963	04 April 1964
Army General Artur da Costa e Silva	04 April 1964	30 June 1966
Marshal Ademar de Queiroz	30 June 1966	15 March 1967
Army General Aurélio de Lyra Tavares	15 March 1967	30 October 1969
Army General Orlando Geisel	30 October 1969	15 March 1974
Army General Vicente de Paulo Dale Coutinho	15 March 1974	27 May 1974
Army General Sylvio Couto Coelho da Frota	27 May 1974	12 October 1977
Army General Fernando Belfort Bethlem	12 October 1977	15 March 1979
Army General Walter Pires de Carvalho e Albuquerque	15 March 1979	15 March 1985

Gallery of Army Ministers from 1963–1985. Top Row, from left to right: Army Generals Jair Dantas Ribeiro and Artur da Costa e Silva, Marshal Ademar de Queiroz, Army Generals Aurélio de Lyra Tavares and Orlando Geisel. Bottom row, from left to right: Army Generals Vicente de Paulo Dale Coutinho, Sylvio Couto Coelho da Frota, Fernando Belfort Bethlem and Walter Pires de Carvalho e Albuquerque. (*Exército Brasileiro*)

Guerrilla (1972–1974). Additionally, between 1956 and 1967, the Brazilian Army participated in the UN Peace Mission in Suez, Egypt.

Regarding the organisation of the Brazilian Army, at the top was the Supreme Commander, a civilian position held by the President of the Republic. Below him was the Army Minister. Next there was an Army General Staff, Land Operations Command, General Department of Personnel, Army Department of Education and Culture, Logistics Command, Department of Engineering and Construction, and finally the Economy and Finance Secretariat. Until 1967, the name of the ministry responsible for managing the Army was the Ministry of War. Between 1967 and 1999, it was renamed the Ministry of the Army.

Subordinated to the Command of Land Operations, the operational arm of the Army was called the *Força Terrestre* (Land Force). This was made up of Army divisions, brigades, combat units and combat support units, which were grouped in military region commands. Table 1 shows the Army Ministers of Brazil between 1963 and 1985.[1]

The Brazilian Army had 11 Military Regions, each one commanded by a major general, as shown in Table 2.[2]

TABLE 2: Brazilian Army Military Regions

Military Region	Headquarters
1°	Rio de Janeiro
2°	São Paulo
3°	Porto Alegre
4°	Juiz de Fora
5°	Curitiba
6°	Salvador
7°	Recife
8°	Belém
9°	Campo Grande
10°	Fortaleza
11°	Brasília

Infantry troops of the Brazilian Army deployed in the city of Rio de Janeiro in 1968 with Mauser rifles and US-style uniform with M1 helmets. This was during the promulgation of Institutional Act No. 5. (*Exército Brasileiro*)

Army troops deployed in M34 REO trucks during student demonstrations against the military regime. (*Exército Brasileiro*)

Brazilian Army officers and NCOs were divided into several arms and specialties: Infantry, Cavalry, Artillery, Engineering, Communications, Logistics, Weapons Maintenance, Vehicle Maintenance, Health Corps, Health Support, Surveyor and Military Band.

The Brazilian Army maintained one of the most structured higher education systems in Brazil, operating in the most diverse branches. Among its main higher education institutions were: The Army Cadet Preparatory School (EsPCEx), Agulhas Negras (Black Needles) Military Academy (AMAN), Officer Improvement School (EsAO), Army Command and General Staff School (ECEME), Military Institute of Engineering (IME), Army Complementary Training School (EsFCEx) and Army Health School (EsSEx).

In addition to these, it had important training centres, such as the Sergeants Weapon School (ESA), the School of Logistics Sergeants (EsSLog), the Sergeants Weapons Improvement School (EASA), the School of Specialised Instruction (EsIE), the Coastal and Anti-Aircraft Artillery School (EsACosAAe), the School of Communications (EsCom), the Army Physical Education School (EsEFEx), the Reserve Officer Preparation Centres (CPOR), the War Sections for the Military Service and the Military Schools.

As for the structure of the Brazilian Army, it was composed of:

- Armies and Commands: There were four Armies and two Commands, each of them commanded by a four-star general (general of the army).
- Divisions: Each Army had divisions, led by a three-star general (major general), which were the main combat units and brought together troops of different specialties.
- Brigades: The brigades were units of mixed composition, commanded by a two-star general (brigadier general) and whose strength varied between 5,000 and 10,000 men.
- Regiments: The brigades had regiments, commanded by a colonel, with three battalions each and between 1,000 and 1,500 troops.
- Battalions: The battalions in turn were made up of three companies that had between 300 and 450 men, commanded by a lieutenant colonel.
- Companies: Each company had three platoons with about 150 men and was commanded by a captain.
- Platoons: The platoons had between 30 and 50 men commanded by a lieutenant.

Appendix I shows the detailed structure and organisation of the Brazilian Army between 1960 and 1980.

While preparing to take part in the Second World War the Brazilian Army acquired 303 half-tracks from the USA within the Lend-Lease Program. These included eight M2s, 75 M2As, and 220 M3/M3A1 and M5s, and remained in service until 1986. Depending on the variant, they were usually armed with a Browning .50cal (12.7mm) heavy machine gun and/or a Colt .30cal (7.62mm) machine gun. (Artwork by David Bocquelet)

A total of 150 M8 Greyhound armoured cars were supplied to the Brazilian Army in 1944 through the Lend-Lease Program. Their primary armament consisted of a 37mm gun, with a .30cal coaxial machine gun and .50cal AA machine gun. In the late 1960s, Brazil developed its own variant (CRR Brasileiro) with an articulated suspension, new gearbox, and a new engine with parts sourced locally. Later on, the type formed the basis for development of an entire family of domestically-designed armoured cars and armoured personnel carriers. (Artwork by David Bocquelet)

In 1942, the USA supplied a total of 44 M4A1 and 10 M4A Sherman medium tanks to the Brazilian Army. These were armed with a 75mm main gun, two .30cal machine guns, and a pintle-mounted Browning .50cal machine gun. Shermans formed the backbone of the Brazilian armoured corps through the 1950s, and the last were withdrawn from service only in the 1970s. (Artwork by David Bocquelet)

Starting in 1944, Brazil was provided with a total of 89 Douglas C-47 transports, and they formed the backbone of the FAB's fleet well into the 1970s. This example (serial number FAB 2018) is shown when operated by the 3° ETA (the 'Pioneer Squadron') in the mid-1970s, when C-47s were still widely used to transport troops and supplies, as well as mail carriers and even as airliners. By this time, the type had been partially replaced by the de Havilland Canada DHC-5 Buffalo, 24 of which were acquired starting in 1968, and by Lockheed C-130 Hercules, a total of 29 of which were purchased staring in 1964. (Artwork by Luca Canossa)

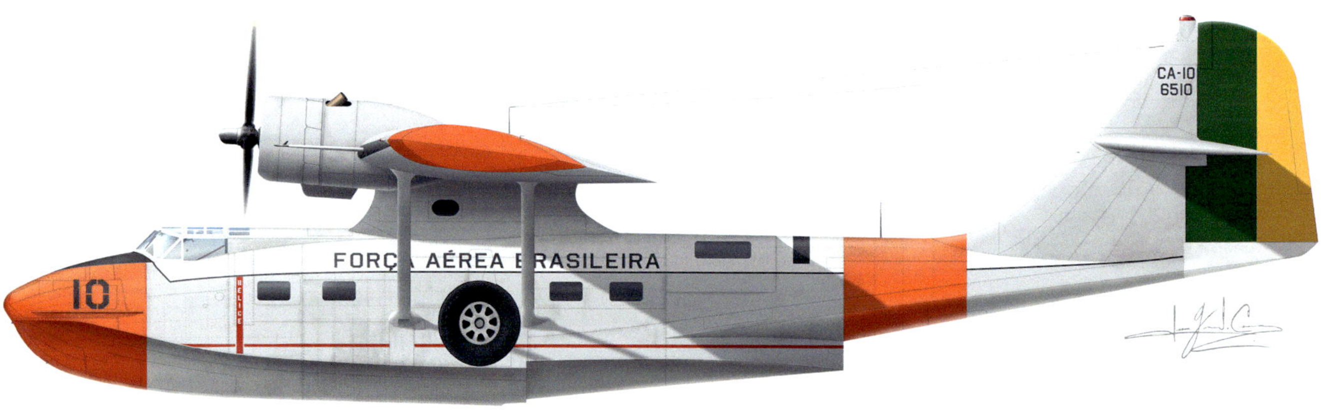

Another classic type obtained by Brazil during the Second World War was the Consolidated PBY-5 Catalina. A total of 7 PBY-5s, 23 PBY-5As, and 3 PBY-5As were acquired starting in 1943, and their survivors remained in operation until 1982. During the 1960s and 1970s they were operated by the 1st Aviation Group, and primarily served as transports in the vast Amazon area, where their amphibious capability was of immense advantage. (Artwork by Luca Canossa)

Brazil acquired a total of 62 Gloster Meteor F.Mk 8 and T.Mk 7 jet fighters, and three different FAB units – including the 1°/1° GAVCA Esquadrão Senta a Púa! of the Second World War-fame – operated them from 1953 until 1974. Single-seat F.Mk 8 fighters were all armed with four internally installed cannon calibre 20mm, but they could also carry bombs and unguided rockets on underwing hardpoints. They were principally left in high-speed silver finish, but regularly wore gaudy markings in the colours of their units, as illustrated on this example with the serial number 4452. (Artwork by Luca Canossa)

The Lockheed T-33 Shooting Star was not the first, but probably the most important, early jet operated by the FAB. A total of 10 T-33As (serials 4310 to 4319) and 48 refurbished AT-33As (4320 to 4367, all drawn from surplus stocks of the USAF) were acquired between 1956 and 1965, all armed with two internally-installed 12.7mm machine guns, and the capability to carry up to two bombs of up to 500kg weight, or up to 10 HVAR unguided 127mm rockets. Initially, AT-33As were left in bare metal overall, as shown here. Unit insignia was usually applied on the rear fuselage, and flight insignia on the nose, while national markings were worn on the wing only. (Artwork by Tom Cooper)

T-33As and AT-33As were operated (in order of their service entry) by the 4th, 14th, and the 1st Aviation Groups and primarily deployed for training- and ground-attack purposes. During local overhauls in the 1960s, the 54 survivors were either overpainted in silver-grey, in light grey, or in white overall. As of 1973-1974, all were concentrated in the 14° GAVCA, home-based at Santos Dumont AB, pending their replacement by Aermacchi MB.326 Xavantess and Northrop F-5E/F Tiger IIs. (Artwork by Tom Cooper)

Starting in May 1958, the 4th Aviation Group at the Fortaleza AB began receiving Lockheed F-80C-10-LO Shooting Star single-seat fighters to replace its obsolete Republic P-47 Thunderbolts. The first batch included 29 jets (serial numbers 4200 to 4228), while four attrition replacements (serials 4229 to 4232) followed in in 1960-1961. Generally, their armament was similar to that of T-33A/AT-33As: the principal difference was four internally-installed 12.7mm machine guns. F-80s remained in service until replaced by AT-26 Xavante light strikers in 1973. (Artwork by Tom Cooper)

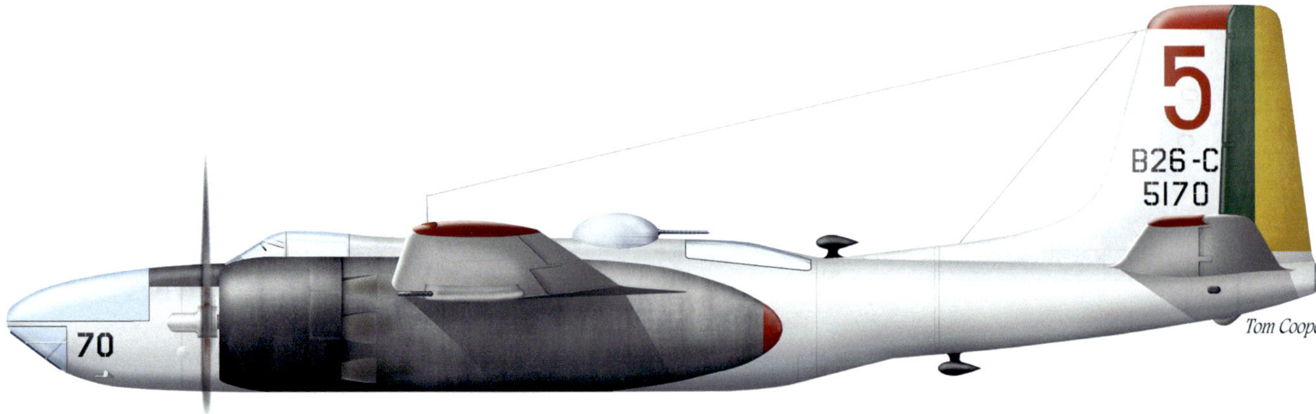

During the Second World War, Brazil acquired a large fleet of Lockheed PV-1 Ventura and PV-2 Harpoons, Boeing B-17Gs, and no fewer than 96 North American B-25 Mitchell medium bombers. When the time came to replace all of these, the country opted to acquire 14 Douglas B-26B and 14 B-26C Invaders (one of which is illustrated here), offered cheaply by Washington. Later on, these were supplemented by four B-26Cs as attrition replacements. The aircraft were initially painted in silver grey overall and served with two squadrons of the 5th Aviation Group. Their principal armament consisted of 12.7mm machine guns (on B-26Cs, these were installed under the wing, inboard of a total of four pylons for unguided rockets), and bombs carried in the bomb bay. (Artwork by Tom Cooper)

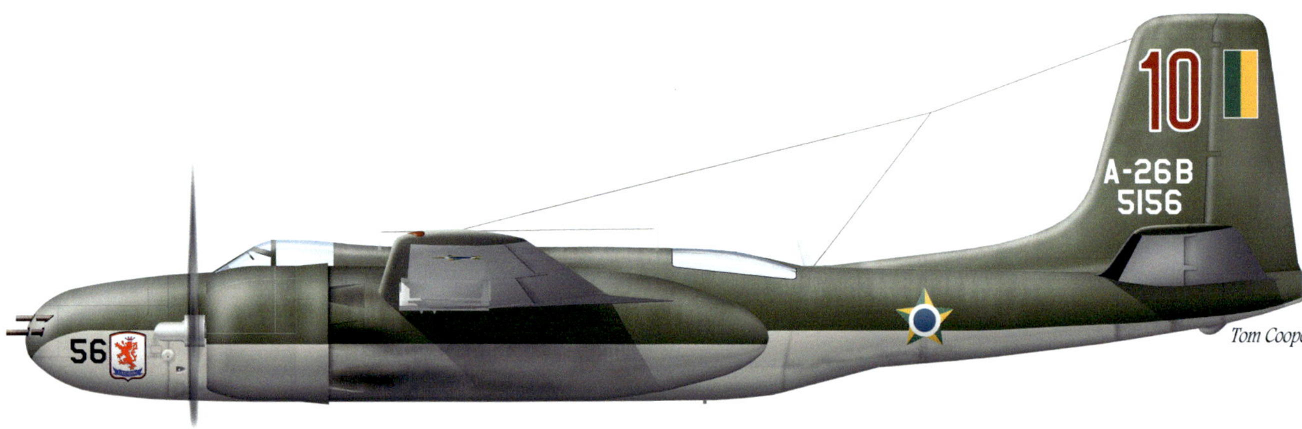

As well by the 5th, the Brazilian B-26s were also operated by the 10th Group, which deployed them as multi-engine trainers and for maritime reconnaissance, as well as undergoing regular attack training with the US Mission in Brazil. In addition to national markings, they wore type designation and serials (5145 to 5158 for B-26Bs, and 5159 to 5176 for B-26Cs) applied in large type on the fin. In 1967-1969, surviving examples underwent an overhaul in the USA, where they received the camouflage pattern in forest green on top and light gray on undersurfaces, similar to that applied on Mark-rebuilt B-26Ks, which is why they were often misidentified as belonging to that version. As can be seen by the designation shown on the vertical tail fin, from 1970 until their withdrawal from use in 1974, all were re-designated as A-26s. (Artwork by Tom Cooper

Concurrent with deliveries of B-26s, in 1957 the USA offered Brazil a squadron worth – 14 – Grumman SA-16 Albatross search and rescue aircraft. Entering service in 1958, they were assigned to the 2nd Squadron of the 10th Aviation Group (a unit also known as the Pelican Squadron) and home-based at Sao Paulo AB. For most of their service, they were left painted in silver grey overall, with large surfaces in dayglo orange, as illustrated here: later on, the upper sides of the cabin and fuselage were re-painted in white, to lessen the effects of the sun. The type was heavily utilised for transport purposes, too, and remained in service until 1980. (Artwork by Tom Cooper)

While the Naval Aviation arm of Brazil was originally established even before an airforce, the two services were amalgamated in 1941 and it was the FAB who operated all maritime patrol aircraft. When the time came to supplant the fleet of such machines acquired during the Second World War, in 1958-1959 Brazil acquired 14 Lockheed Neptune MR.MK 1s (P2V-5) from the Royal Air Force. Designated P-15 in FAB service, they were assigned to the 7th Aviation Group, based at Salvador, and received serials 7000 to 7013. Illustrated here is the P-15 with serial number 7013 (ex RAF WX556), which on 8-9 December 1961 set the South American endurance record when remaining airborne for 24 hours and 35 minutes. (Artwork by Tom Cooper)

In 1970, Brazil acquired four Sikorsky S-61D-3 Sea King helicopters (N3007, N3008, N3009 and N3010), roughly equivalent to the US Navy's SH-3D. Followed by two additional examples (N3011 and N2012, shown here) they were operated by the Esquadron de Helicopteros de Emprego Geral (HS-1), home-based at Sao Pedro da Aldeia but often deployed aboard the aircraft carrier *Minas Gerais*. Augmented by four Italian-built S-61Ds and then by two ex-US Navy SH-3Ds, the entire fleet was subsequently overhauled and upgraded to the same standard, including intake filters, under-nose radar and compatibility with the French-made Aérospatiale AM.39 Exocet anti-ship missiles, which made them the most potent sub-variant of Sea King operated in South America. (Artwork by Tom Cooper)

For service on its destroyers of Gearing and Allen M. Sumner classes, and the Niterói class frigates, between 1966 and 1977 the re-established Brazilian Naval Aviation acquired a total of 10 Westland Wasps ex-Royal Navy. Designated the UH-2 and UH-2A in Brazil, they were assigned to the 1° Esquadrao de Helicópteros de Emprego Geral (HU-1). While primarily equipped for anti-submarine purposes, they also saw heavy deployment for utility tasks, and remained in service until 1991. (Artwork by Tom Cooper)

Aiming to replace its T-6s, in 1970 Brazil acquired two Aermacchi MB.326, and then obtained the licence for production of 166 MB.326GCs. Following full technology transfer, production was launched in 1971 using 38 kits provided by Aeromacchi, and the new jet entered service with the FAB under the designation AT-26 Xavante. By 1973-1975, they were operated by the 1°/4° EMRA, 2°/5° EMRA, and the 1° and 3°/10° GAVCA. Xavantes had no internally-installed armament, but could be armed with pods for 12.7mm machine guns (shown here), pods for unguided 68mm rockets, and also carry underwing drop tanks. Unit insignia was frequently (but not always) applied on the fuselage below the front cockpit. (Artwork by Tom Cooper)

In 1969, the FAB intended to acquire the McDonnell-Douglas F-4 Phantom II. However, US arms-exports policy forced the Brazilians to look elsewhere, and in May 1970, an order was placed for 12 Dassault Mirage IIIEBR single-seaters, and four Mirage IIIDBR two-seat conversion trainers. Entering service under the designation F-103E and F-103D, respectively, they were assigned to the 1° ALADA at Anápolis air base, and served as interceptors armed with Matra R.530 semi-active radar-homing- (shown as installed under the centreline), and infrared-homing air-to-air missiles, as well as two internally-installed DEFA 30mm cannons. Additional Mirages were acquired in the 1980s, but were all second-hand aircraft from surplus stocks of the French air force. (Artwork by Tom Cooper)

In 1974, Brazil renewed negotiations for a US-made fighter jet, and was eventually granted permission to acquire 37 single-seat Northrop F-5E- and six two-seat F-5F Tiger IIs, thus becoming the first export customer for this type in Latin America. The example shown here (serial FAB 4820) was the first single-seater to reach Brazil: it entered service with the 1° GAVCA. All the Brazilian Tigers originally wore the South-East Asia camouflage pattern in tan and two shades of green, as shown here. Their principal armament consisted of two internally-installed Colt Mk. 12 20mm guns, and AIM-9 Sidewinder infrared air-to-air missiles. For ground attacks, they could be armed with US-designed bombs such as the Mk.82 (shown as installed under the wing), which were also manufactured under licence in Brazil. (Artwork by Tom Cooper)

(Map by Author)

(Map by Author)

Brazilian Army tanks: M3A1 Stuart (top left), M4A1 Sherman (top right) and M41 Walker Bulldogs (bottom left and right). (Hélio Higuchi collection)

Two locally manufactured armoured vehicles: Engesa EE-09 Cascavel M1/M2 with Cockerill 90mm gun (left) and Engesa EE-11 Urutú personnel carrier (right). (*Exército Brasileiro*)

The variety of tanks and armoured vehicles in service with the Brazilian Army are shown in Table 3.[3]

TABLE 3: Brazilian Army Tanks and Armoured Vehicles

Vehicle	Quantity	Years in service
M3/M3A1 Stuart light tank	437	1941–1972
M3A3/M3A5 Lee medium tank	104	1942–1969
M4 Sherman NDV	10	1942–1978
M3A1 scout car	90	1942–1986

M2/M2A half-track armoured vehicle	8/75	1942–1986
M3/M3A1/M5 half-track armoured vehicle	220	1942–1986
Ford M8 Greyhound armoured car	150	1944–1987
Ford M20 command armoured car	20	1944–1986
T17 Deerhound armoured car	54	1945–1946
M4/M4A1 Sherman medium tank with 75mm gun	39	1945–1978
M4 Sherman composite hull	34	1945–1978
M39 armoured utility vehicle	15	1945–1946
M26 tank transporter	5	1945–1946
M4A1 high-speed tractor	64	1949–1997
M32 recovery vehicle	2	1953–1980
M41 Walker Bulldog tank	160	1960–1967
M41A1/M41A3 Walker Bulldog tank with 76mm gun	300/55	1960–1982
M59A1 VBTT armoured personnel carrier	20	1960–1982
M74 armoured recovery vehicle	2	1960–1982
M108 self-propelled 105mm howitzer	72	1960–2017
FMC M113AO armoured personnel carrier	584	1965–1988
M578 light recovery vehicle	17	1971–present
Engesa EE-09 Cascavel M1/M2 armoured car with Cockerill 90mm gun	600	1974–present
Engesa EE-11 Urutú armoured personnel carrier	250	1976–present
VBC-CC MB-2 Lag X1A1/X2 Carcará armoured fighting vehicle	53/24	1976–1994
VBE L Pnt XLP-10 Lag bridge launcher	5	1976–1978
Marder 1A2 SAM Roland II System	4	1977–2001

In the late 1960s and early 1970s, the Brazilian Army had a total of 170,000 effectives, including officers, non-commissioned officers and troops, but in the mid-80s it would reach the figure of 194,380 effectives.

From the Second World War onwards, American influence in the Brazilian Army was characterised by the use of US combat doctrine, the type of uniform, helmets, small and large arms, tanks and armoured vehicles. This influence lasted a long time and continued during the military regimes between 1964 and 1985, although Brazil did begin to develop its own military industry.

In the 1960s, when modern armies were fully motorised and mechanised, these technologies coexisted in Brazil with horses still being used for both mounted cavalry and transportation tasks. In practice, mounted cavalry requisitioned civilian vehicles when necessary. The armoured vehicles were all American: M8 Greyhound, M20 and M3A1 scout car armoured cars, M2, M2A1, M3, M3A1 and M5 half-tracks, and M3 and M3A1 Stuart, M4 Sherman and M41 Walker Bulldog tanks. This external dependence made maintenance and parts replacement difficult. The Brazilian Army also had a large number of trucks and utility vehicles, as shown in Table 4.[4]

Utility vehicles and trucks of the Brazilian Army: Ford M151 MUTT equipped with an M40 recoilless gun (above left), Willys MB Jeep (above right), Mercedes-Benz L1213 (below left) and REO M34 (below right). (Hélio Higuchi collection)

TABLE 4: Brazilian Army Trucks and Utility Vehicles		
Vehicle	**Quantity**	**Years in service**
GMC CCKW 352B2 truck	2,520	1941–1986
Studebaker US6 G630 truck	808	1942–1969
Diamond T968/T969 6x6 truck	38/15	1942–1961
Dodge WC62/WC63 Big Shot 6x6 truck	137	1942–1978
Corbitt US White cargo truck	109	1944–1971
GMC CCKW 353C2/D1 truck	127	1944–1978
Opel Blitz II truck	308	1951–1973
M26 Dragon Wagon truck	1	1954–1970
FNM-Alfa Romeo D-9500/D-11000 truck	1,380	1957–1987
Chevrolet Brasil 6400/6500 truck	820	1958–1971
Ford F-600 truck	1,690	1958–1978
Ford-Engesa F-600 truck	2,850	1958–2004
REO M34 G742 truck	980	1958–2004
Mercedes-Benz LP-321/331 truck	620	1960–1981
FNM-Alfa Romeo Mechanical Horse truck	112	1961–1989
Mercedes-Benz Unimog truck	978	1962–present
Chevrolet C-60/D-60 truck	892	1964–1994
Chevrolet-Engesa C-60/D-60 truck	1,210	1966–1997
Mercedes-Benz L-1111/1213/1114 truck	1,580	1966–2002
Mercedes-Benz/Engesa Series L/LG Mamute truck	4,500	1970–present
Dodge-Chrysler Series D truck	690	1971–1994
Scania 110 Super 6x6 VTTNE truck	125	1972–2008
Dodge WC51/52 Beep utility vehicle	954	1942–1976
Dodge WC54 ambulance	149	1942–1978
Dodge WC56/57 command car	223	1942–1981
Jeep-Ford GPA 4x4 utility vehicle	104	1942–1970
Jeep-Ford GPW 4x4 utility vehicle	1,985	1942–1970
Willys MB Jeep 4x4 utility vehicle	32	1942–1970
Jeep CJ-5/6 WOB 4x4 utility vehicle	2,850	1959–present
Volkswagen Kombi van	2,282	1961–present
Volkswagen Kombi pick-up utility vehicle	650	1964–present
MUTT M151A1/M151A1C utility vehicle (jeep)	108	1965–2002
Toyota Bandeirante utility vehicle	1,470	1965–present
Dodge M37/M43 4x4 utility vehicle	332	1966–1997
Chevrolet Veraneio C-1416/C-1410 utility vehicle	1,512	1966–1988
Chevrolet-Engesa C10/C14/C15 utility vehicle	988	1974–1998
Gurgel X-10 Xavante/X-12 Tocantins utility vehicle	910	1975–2004
Gurgel X-15/X-20 utility vehicle	58	1979–1998

Brazilian Army manoeuvres in the late 1960s: an M41 Walker Bulldog tank with several M113s (left) and soldiers practicing shooting with FN MAG medium machine guns. An M8 Greyhound can be seen in the background (right). (Hélio Higuchi collection)

Brazilian Army small arms in the 1960s included Colt M1911A1 and Smith & Wesson M1917 pistols, INA 1950 and 1953 submachine guns, and Madsen 1917 and Browning M1919 machine guns. The bolt-action Mauser 1908 and Itajubá M954 Carabiner rifles were also used. With modernisation came NATO-style standardisation, using the 9x19mm Parabellum calibres for pistols (Colt M1911A1 model 1973 and Beretta 1975) and submachine guns (Beretta 1972), and 7.62x51mm for rifles and machine guns (FN FAL, FN FAP and FN MAG).

After 1970, the regiments were abolished, freeing up their battalions. There was considerable motorisation and mechanisation, with the vehicle fleet dominated by the national automobile industry supplying unarmoured vehicles such as trucks. Most infantry battalions became motorised, although the change was only in transportation, as combat continued to be on foot. The number of Armoured Infantry Battalions (*Batalhão de Infantaria Blindado*, BIB) went from two to seven, adopting the M113 armoured personnel carrier. There was the special category of Airborne Infantry Battalions, then Parachute Battalions, and the new category of Jungle Infantry Battalions. Light Tank Battalions (*Batalhões de Carro de Combate Leve*, BCCL) were converted into BIBs. Several cavalry regiments continued to use horses in the 1960s, but that gradually changed with the acquisition of armoured vehicles and tanks.

In the 1960s, Brazilian field artillery replaced their 332 German 75mm Krupp guns with 320 American 105mm M101 and 19 M102 howitzers, while the medium artillery used 146 American 155mm M114s. The Brazilian Army received 36 57mm M1 and 148 37mm M3/M3A1 anti-tank guns. Brazil's anti-aircraft artillery replaced German 88mm guns with American 40mm and 90mm ones, but all were already obsolete due to the advent of the jet plane. The existing AA groups were for the defence of the interior, and the campaigning divisions did not have any anti-aircraft support. Brazilian coastal artillery, a branch considered obsolete, used 99 British 152.4mm (6-inch) Vickers-Armstrong guns. In the mid-1960s, 210 106mm M40A1 recoilless guns were acquired. There were howitzer regiments, theoretically with three groups, but none of them were complete, and independent groups of cannons and howitzers. In the 1970s, the Army acquired Italian OTO Melara Mod. 56 howitzers, dismantlable and easy to transport, for paratroopers and jungle units, and the American 105mm M108 tracked howitzer, capable of following the movement of armoured units. Self-propelled artillery was a great advance for the Army, but abroad the M108 was already considered outdated in range and firepower when purchased.

The number of combat engineering and communications units grew. Those accompanying the armoured brigades received their own armoured vehicles. Supply, transport, health, maintenance and service activities were centralised in new Logistics Battalions (B-Log).

Finally, regarding the Army Aviation, the Military Aviation belonged to the Army from 1918 to 1941, when the FAB was created (see below) and all aircraft, flying and maintenance personnel were transferred to the air force. It was in 1986 that the modern Army Aviation (AvEx) was created, but only with helicopters, although in the near future at the time of writing they could acquire fixed-wing training, liaison and transport aircraft.

Brazilian Air Force (*Força Aérea Brasileira*, FAB)

The Brazilian Air Force (FAB) was created as an arm independent of the Army with the creation of the Ministry of Aeronautics on 20 January 1941. All personnel and flight equipment of both the Army and Naval Aviation became part of the new air force. From 1941–1999, the highest aeronautical authority was the Minister of Aeronautics.

The FAB participated actively in the Second World War both in Italy and the South Atlantic, fighting with the Allied forces. The FAB received hundreds of new combat, transport and training aircraft through the American government's Lend-Lease programme. The FAB units deployed to Italy in 1944 were the 1st Fighter Aviation Group (1° *Grupo de Aviação de Caça*, GAvCA) with Republic P-47 Thunderbolt fighters and the 1st Liaison and Observation Squadron (1° *Esquadrilha de Ligação e Observação*, 1° ELO) with Piper Cub L-4H aircraft, fighting alongside the United States Army Air Forces.

After the war, the FAB began flying the British Gloster Meteor FMk.8 fighter jet. These were purchased from the British in exchange for 15,000 tons of raw cotton, as Brazil had no foreign currency reserves to spare. The jets were operated by the FAB until the early 1970s. In the mid-1950s, Lockheed F-80Cs and TF-33As were acquired, which were replaced by Embraer EMB-326/AT-26 Xavante, Dassault Mirage IIIEBR/DBR and Northrop F-5E/B jets in the 1970s.

The FAB officers who were in charge of the Ministry of Aeronautics between 1963 and 1985 are listed in Table 5.[5]

The general structure of the Ministry of Aeronautics, on which the FAB depended, was organised as follows:

- General Management Bodies: Aeronautics High Command and Aeronautics General Staff.
- Management Body: Department of Civil Aeronautics.
- Advisory Bodies: Superior Council of Aeronautics, General Inspectorate of Aeronautics, Cabinet of the Minister, Legal Consulting, Councils and Commissions.
- Support Bodies: Directorates, Services, Institutes, Sub departments and other bodies subordinated to the general commands and the Department of Civil Aeronautics.

Ministers of Aeronautics from 1962–1985. Top row, from left to right: Air Major Brigadiers Reynaldo Joaquim Ribeiro de Carvalho Filho and Anísio Botelho, Air Lieutenant Brigadier Francisco de Assis Corrêa de Mello, and Air Major Brigadiers Nelson Freire Lavenére-Wanderley and Márcio de Souza e Mello. Bottom row, from left to right Air Marshals Eduardo Gomes and Márcio de Souza e Mello, and Air Lieutenant Brigadiers Joelmir Campos de Araripe Macedo and Délio Jardim de Mattos. (FAB)

TABLE 5: Ministers of Aeronautics 1963–1985

Minister	Years
Air Major Brigadier Reynaldo Joaquim Ribeiro de Carvalho Filho	17 September 1962 – 14 June 1963
Air Major Brigadier Anísio Botelho	14 June 1963 – 04 April 1964
Air Lieutenant Brigadier Francisco de Assis Corrêa de Mello	04 April 1964 – 20 April 1964
Air Major Brigadier Nelson Freire Lavenére-Wanderley	20 April 1964 – 15 December 1964
Air Major Brigadier Márcio de Souza e Mello	15 December 1964 – 09 January 1965
Air Marshal Eduardo Gomes	09 January 1965 – 15 March 1967
Air Marshal Márcio de Souza e Mello	15 March 1967 – 25 November 1971
Air Lieutenant Brigadier Joelmir Campos de Araripe Macedo	25 November 1971 – 15 March 1979
Air Lieutenant Brigadier Délio Jardim de Mattos	15 March 1979 – 15 March 1985

- Brazilian Air Force: General Air Command (COMGAR), General Staff Command, General Support Command (COMGAP), General Investigation and Development Command (COMPED) and Regional Air Commands (COMAR).

The General Air Command was responsible for the preparation and efficient use of the FAB air units' operations. It was made up of the Commander, General Staff, Headquarters bodies and large units. The Commander General was an active FAB lieutenant brigadier.

The major units of the FAB were:

- Coastal Command (COMCOS), which carried out maritime reconnaissance and SAR missions.
- Aerotactical Command (COMAT), in charge of all offensive and defensive air operations in coordination with the Army and Navy.
- Air Transport Command (COMTA), in charge of military air transport operations and national air mail (CAN).
- Air Defence Command (COMDA), which carried out air defence operations throughout the territory in coordination with the other armed forces.

The aircraft types in active service in the FAB between 1963 and 1985 are listed in Appendix II. The FAB's Regional Command zones and bases are listed in Table 6.[6]

A flight line of FAB Gloster Meteor F-8 fighters (left). A Gloster Meteor TF-7 advanced trainer (right). They were the first jets in Brazil's air force. (Mauro Lins de Barros; FAB)

An FAB Lockheed F-80C Shooting Star tactical fighter in the 1960s (left). A Lockheed AT-33A advanced trainer (right). (FAB)

FAB Embraer EMB-326GB/AT-26 Xavante advanced trainers and attack aircraft, and licence-built Aermacchi MB-326 (top). A good number of North American T-6D Texans were still in service in the FAB in the late 1960s and early 1970s. (Col. Camazano collection)

The FAB still had a good number of the veteran Douglas B-26 Invaders active in the 1960s; they were only withdrawn from service in the mid-70s. The B-26B Invader flight line (top). An A-26C Invader with the bomb bay doors open (bottom). (FAB)

An FAB Dassault Mirage IIIEBR interceptor fighter from the 1st ALADA Squadron. These Mirages were known as F-103Es in the Brazilian Air Force (left). A Mirage IIIDBR getting ready for a training flight (right). (FAB)

An FAB Northrop F-5E dropping Mk.82 bombs (left). A Northrop F-5B advanced trainer (right). (FAB)

Flight line of Cessna T-37C Tweety Birds at the Air Force Academy (AFA) in Pirassununga in the 1970s (left). An AFA Cessna T-37C Tweety Bird with tip tanks. (FAB)

TABLE 6: FAB Regional Air Commands

COMAR	Bases	Squadrons
I	Belém AFB (BABE)	1° ETA and 1° EMRA
II	Fortaleza AFB (BAFZ)	1°/4° GAV
	Natal AFB (BANT)	5° GAV, 1°/5° GAV, 1° EIA, 2° EIA, 3° EIA, CFPM, CATRE
	Salvador AFB (BASV)	1°/7° GAV
	Recife AFB (BARF)	1°/6° GAV, 2° ETA, 2°/8° GAV, 2° EMRA
III	Galeão AFB (BAGL)	1°/1° GT, 1°/2° GT, 2°/2° GT, 3° ETA, CECAN
	Santa Cruz AFB (BASC)	1° GAVCA, 1° GAE, 3° EMRA, 1°/13° GAV, 1° ECA
	Dos Afonsos AFB (BAAF)	1° GTT, EAS, 3°/8° GAV

IV	Campo Grande AFB (BACG)	1°/15° GAV, 2°/10° GAV
	Santos AFB (BAST)	CIEH, 1°/11° GAV
	São Paulo AFB (BASP)	1°/10° GAV, 2°/10° GAV, 4° EMRA, 4° ETA
	AFA – Pirassununga, SP	EDA, EIA
V	Santa María AFB (BASM)	5° EMRA, 5°/8° GAV, 3°/10° GAV, 1°/10° GAV
	Florianópolis AFB (BAFL)	2°/10° GAV, 2°/7° GAV
	Canoas AFB (BACO)	1°/14° GAV, 1° ERA, 3° ELO, 5° ETA, 2° ECA
VI	Brasília AFB (BABR)	GTE, 6° ETA
	Anápolis AFB (BAAN)	1° GDA, 1° ALADA
	Brig. Velloso Testing Ground (CPBV)	-
VII	Boa Vista AFB (BABV)	1°/3° GAV
	Manaos AFB (BAMN)	1°/9° GAV, 7° ETA, 7°/8° GAV
	Porto Velho AFB (BAPV)	-
	Boa Vista AFB (BABV)	-
Formations are listed by Squadron and then Group, for example 1°/4° GAV: 1st Squadron of the 4th Aviation Group. In 1969, the ERA groups were reorganised into three squadrons: 1° ERA in Canoas, 2° ERA in São Paulo and 3° ERA in Rio de Janeiro. In 1972, they were renamed as EMRA (Mixed Reconnaissance and Attack Squadron).		
Note: Between 1957 and 1998, the FAB operated the Embarked Air Group (1° GAE) with two squadrons, 1°/1° GAE and 2°/1° GAE, aboard the aircraft carrier A-11 *Minas Gerais* of the Brazilian Navy.		

Some FAB transport aircraft (clockwise from top left): Lockheed C-130E Hercules, Douglas C-118 Liftmaster, Douglas C-47 and De Havilland Canada DHC-5 Buffalo. (R.A. Scholefield & FAB via Hélio Higuchi)

Some of the helicopter types in service with the FAB in the 1960s and 1970s (clockwise from top left): Bell UH-1D, Bell UH-1H, Bell 47G.2 and Bell 206B Jet Ranger. (Col. Camazano collection)

(Clockwise from top left): FAB Grumman SA-16A Albatross, PBY-6A Catalina, Lockheed P2V-5 Neptune and Grumman S-2A Tracker landing on the Brazilian Navy's aircraft carrier MB *Minas Gerais*. (FAB & Leonardo Carvalho)

The ERA squadrons and then the EMRA had North American T-6G Texan advanced training aircraft and North American T-6D Texan attack aircraft, the latter widely used in the fight against the Araguaia Guerrilla in the early 1970s. (FAB)

On 18 July 1965, the Reconnaissance and Attack Squadrons (*Esquadrilhas de Recononhecimento e Ataque*, ERA) were created, which were equipped with North American T-6Gs for training and T-6D Texan aircraft for armed operations. Years later, these squadrons would be key in the fight against the *Araguaia Guerrilla*. Initially, there were five detachments: ERA 21 in Recife, ERA 31 in Santa Cruz, ERA 41 in São Paulo, ERA 51 in Canoas and ERA 61 in Brasília.

Some years later, various changes were made and more detachments were added: ERA 21 in Natal, ERA 31 in Santa Cruz, ERA 32 in Barbacena, ERA 41 in São Paulo, ERA 42 in Campo Grande, ERA 51 in Canoas and ERA 61 in Brasília. The ERA squadrons participated in several training operations: Operation Poti in 1965 in the northeast (II COMAR), Operation Charrúa in 1966 in the south (V COMAR) and Operation Xavante in 1967 in Mato Grosso do Sul, which was a combined exercise with the Army and Navy.

By 1970, the ERAs were reorganised into three squadrons, with 1° ERA in Canoas with two detachments (ERA-42 and ERA-51), 2° ERA in São Paulo with three detachments (ERA-32, ERA-41 and ERA-61) and 3° ERA in Santa Cruz with two detachments (ERA-21 and ERA-31). Between 1970 and 1972, the ERA squadrons participated in five operations:

- *Operação Jacupiranda* in the state of São Paulo in 1970 in support of the Army against a small guerrilla concentration, with six armed T-6Ds.
- *Operação Comendo Pó* (Operation Eating Dust) in 1970 in the Brasília area, which involved tactical training.
- *Operação Carajás* in 1970 in the Marabá area, a large-scale counterinsurgency exercise in the same area that the actual combat against the *Araguaia Guerrilla* would take place two years later.
- *Operação Pinguim* (Operation Penguin) in 1971 in the São Jerónimo area, Rio Grande do Sul, with eight armed T-6Ds involved in shooting, bombing and rocket-launching practice.
- *Operação Papagaio* (Operation Parrot) in 1972, together with the Army and Navy, in the Marabá and Xambioá area, which was a real operation against the *Araguaia Guerrilla*, which is described in the corresponding chapter.

Between 1971 and 1973, the ERA squadrons evolved to become Mixed Reconnaissance and Attack Squadrons (Esquadrao Misto de Reconhecimento e Ataque, EMRA). The new organisation consisted of five squadrons:

- 1° EMRA, at Belém AFB (BABE), known as *Esquadrão Falcão* (Falcon Squadron), with T-6D/Gs, Bell UH-1Hs and Cessna L-19A/Es.
- 2° EMRA, at Recife AFB (BARF), known as *Esquadrão Poti* (Poti Squadron), with Bell Jet Rangers, Neiva L-42 Regentes, Bell UH-1Hs and T-6D/Gs.
- 3° EMRA, at Santa Cruz AFB (BASC), known as *Esquadrão Águia* (Eagle Squadron), with T-6D/Gs, Bell Jet Rangers, Bell UH-1Hs, Neiva L-42 Regente and Cessna L-19A/Es.
- 4° EMRA, at São Paulo AFB (BASP), known as *Esquadrão Dragão* (Dragon Squadron), with T-6D/Gs, Neiva L-42 Regentes and Bell UH-1Hs.
- 5° EMRA, at Santa María AFB (BASM), known as *Esquadrão Pantera* (Panther Squadron), with Cessna L-19A/Es, Bell Jet Rangers, T-6D/Gs, Neiva L-42 Regentes and Bell UH-1Ds.

In 1972, in order to control Brazilian airspace, the First Integrated Centre for Air Defence and Air Traffic Control (CINDACTA 1) was created, based in Brasília. This system ensured the defence of the airspace of the Federal District (*Distrito Federal*, DF) and the southeastern region. With the passage of time, it would be possible to cover all of the country's airspace with three other systems,

Two types of light aircraft used in EMRA squadrons: the locally manufactured Neiva L-42 Regente (left) and Cessna 305A/L-19A Bird Dog (right), which were used as forward air controllers and also on liaison missions. (Col. Camazano collection)

A Brazilian Air Force Boeing B-17G flying over the French Navy destroyer D-636 *Tartu* in 1963. Brazilian Navy warships underway, heading northwards in formation, during the Lobster War with France in 1963 (left). From top to bottom, destroyers D-30 MB *Pernambuco* and D-29 MB *Paraná,* light cruiser C-12 MB *Tamandaré*, and destroyers D-27 MB *Pará* and D-28 MB *Paraíba* (right). (FAB & Marinha do Brasil)

Between 1964 and 1985, the Brazilian Ministers of the Navy were, from left to right, Admirals Augusto Hamann Rademaker Grünewald and Paulo Bosísio, Squadron Admirals Zilmar Campos de Araripe Macedo, Adalberto de Barros Nunes, Geraldo Azevedo Henning, Maximiano Eduardo da Silva Fonseca and Alfredo Karam. (*Marinha do Brasil*)

CINDACTA 2 (Curitiba), 3 (Recife) and 4 (Manaos). Also from that year on, EMBRAER (*Empresa Brasileira de Aeronáutica S.A.*, Brazilian Aeronautics Company, Inc.) began to manufacture the EMB-326 Xavante under license from Italy, which would replace the old Lockheed F-80/AT-33A jets then in service in the FAB. Years later, EMBRAER would manufacture its own civil, commercial and military aircraft designs.

The FAB also had a series of utility vehicles and trucks: Chevrolet-Engesa C10/C14/C15, Chevrolet 6500, Chevrolet C60/D60, Dodge-Chrysler Brasil, Dodge M37, Dodge WC51/52 Beep, Dodge WC53, Dodge WC54 Ambulance, Dodge WC56/57, FNM-Alfa Romeo Mechanical Horse, FNM-Alfa Romeo D9500/D11000, Ford F600, Ford-Engesa F600, GMC CCKW 353B2, GMC 353C2, GMC Veraneio, Gurgel X-10/X-12, Jeep-Ford GPW, Willys CJ-5 Jeep, Willys MB 1942 Jeep, Volkswagen Kombi van/Kombi pick-up, Mercedes-Benz 1519/1819, Mercedes-Benz L1111, Mercedes-Benz Unimog, Willys F85 Rural and Toyota Bandeirante.

Brazilian Navy (*Marinha do Brasil*, MB)

The Brazilian Navy, which was officially born with the country's independence in 1822, has had a long tradition in defence of its coastal waters of the Atlantic Ocean and the mighty rivers that irrigate this enormous country. It has long been the largest naval force in Latin America, given Brazil's territorial extent.

The Brazilian Navy has participated in several conflicts with its naval force: Independence War (1821–1824), Confederation of Equador (1824), Cisplatina War (1825–1828), Cabanagem (1835–1840), War of the Farrapos (1835–1845), Balaiada (1835–1841), Prata War (1851–1852), Uruguayan War (1864–1865), Paraguayan War (1864–1870), Navy Revolt (1893–1894), Federalist Revolution (1893–1895), First World War (1917–1918), Constitutional Revolution (1932), Second World War (1942–1945), Lobster War against France (1962–1963) and the Araguaia Guerrilla (1972–1974).

In the early 1960s, an event would take place that would become known as the *Guerra da Lagosta* (Lobster War). French fishing boats began fishing off the coast of Pernambuco, looking for lobster, which had been eradicated in traditional French fishing locations. However, Brazilian lobster was the source of an income of almost $3 million a year. The first French boats began fishing in Brazilian waters in 1961, with authorisation, but after it was discovered that they were fishing on an industrial scale, the Brazilian Navy cancelled the license. The navies of Brazil and France were mobilised to the area, but no naval combat took place and the conflict of interests was finally resolved diplomatically. France then requested authorisation to fish outside Brazilian territorial waters, in the continental shelf region, and authorisation was again granted. Between 1967 and 1974, the Brazilian Navy also participated in operations in what became known as the *Araguaia Guerrilla*.

Just like the Army and the FAB, the Brazilian Navy had its own ministry, which was under the command of the Minister of the Navy. The naval officers who were in charge of the Navy Ministry between 1964 and 1985 are listed in Table 7.[7]

TABLE 7: Brazilian Navy Ministers

Minister	Years
Admiral Augusto Hamann Rademaker Grünewald	04 April 1964 – 20 April 1964
Squadron Admiral Ernesto de Mello Baptista	20 April 1964 – 15 January 1965
Admiral Paulo Bosísio	15 January 1965 – 17 December 1965
Squadron Admiral Zilmar Campos de Araripe Macedo	17 December 1965 – 15 March 1967
Admiral Augusto Hamann Rademaker Grünewald	15 March 1967 – 30 October 1969
Squadron Admiral Adalberto de Barros Nunes	30 October 1969 – 15 March 1974
Squadron Admiral Geraldo Azevedo Henning	15 March 1974 – 15 March 1979
Squadron Admiral Maximiano Eduardo da Silva Fonseca	15 March 1979 – 21 March 1984
Squadron Admiral Alfredo Karam	21 March 1984 – 15 March 1985

The sea and river fleet of the Brazilian Navy had on strength between 1964 and 1985: one aircraft carrier, two light cruisers, 28 destroyers, six frigates, 10 corvettes, 10 minesweepers, six sub-hunters, 12 submarines, six coastal patrol ships, five river patrol boats, one river monitor, one river transport ship, five training vessels, two hospital ships, 11 ocean tugs, four port tugs, six tugs, four transport ships, four troop transport ships, two gasoline tankers, eight hydrographic vessels, 10 beacon ships, four LCUs (Landing Craft Utility) and 34 LCVPs (Landing Craft, Vehicle, Personnel) as detailed in Appendix III.

The Naval Districts and their bases were organised as shown in Table 8.[8]

TABLE 8: Brazilian Navy Districts and Bases

Naval District	City	Naval Base
1º	Rio de Janeiro	Navy Arsenal
		Rio de Janeiro Naval Base
		Submarine Base in Madeira Island
		São Pedro da Aldeia Naval Air Base
		Almirante Castro e Silva Naval Base
2º	Salvador	Aratú Naval Base
3º	Natal	Natal Naval Base
4º	Belém	Val-de-Cães Naval Base
5º	Rio Grande	-
6º	Ladário	Ladário River Base
7º	Brasília	-
8º	São Paulo	-
9º	Manáus	Amazonas Naval Station

The Navy and Marines had the following types of trucks and utility vehicles: Toyota Bandeirante, Willys F85 Rural, Mercedes Benzl LP-231/331, Mercedez Benz L-1111, Mercedes-Benz 1519/1819, Ford M151 MUTT, Willys MB 1942 Jeep, Willys CJ-5 Jeep, Jeep-Ford GPW, Volkswagen Kombi/Kombi Pick-up, Gurgel X-10/X-12, GMC Veraneio, GMC CCKW 353C2, GMC CCKW 353B2, Ford-Engesa F600, Ford F600, FNM-Alfa Romeo D9500/D11000, GMC-Biselli DUKW truck, Dodge WC51/52, Dodge M37, Chevrolet-Engesa C60/D60, Chevrolet 6500 and Chevrolet-Engesa C10/C14/C15.

Marine Corps (*Corpo de Fuzileiros Navais*, CFN)

The Marine Corps, created in 1808 when Brazil was still a Portuguese colony, is the Brazilian Navy's integral force responsible for land combat. The Corps specialises in amphibious warfare. It has been based throughout the national territory, both on the coast and in the riverside regions of the Amazon and the *Pantanal* (wetlands), in addition to the Caatinga (in northeastern Brazil) and other regions. Acting in times of peace to secure the Navy's installations, it has supported security forces and helped needy populations through civic-social actions developed regionally by the Naval Districts. Abroad, it oversees the security of Brazilian embassies in Algeria, Paraguay, Haiti and Bolivia. It has participated in all the armed conflicts in the history of Brazil, both external and internal.

The Corps had its own armoured, transport and utility vehicles (SK-105 Kürassier, M113, Mowag Piranha, Mercedes Benz Unimog, Toyota Bandeirante, MBB 1720), howitzers (M114, L118), mortars

The Brazilian Navy's Colossus class aircraft carrier A11 MB *Minas Gerais* (former Royal Navy R71 HMS *Vengeance*). Seven Grumman S-2 Trackers from the FAB's 1° GAE Squadron can be seen on the flight deck. (*Marinha do Brasil*)

Two Niterói class frigates, F40 MB *Niterói* and F41 MB *Defensora*, both with a helicopter deck and missile launchers. (*Marinha do Brasil*)

The two Brooklyn class light cruisers of the Brazilian Navy, C11 MB *Almirante Barroso* (former US Navy CL-41 USS *Philadelphia*) and C12 *Almirante Marquês de Tamandaré* (former US Navy CL-49 USS *St. Louis*). (*Marinha do Brasil*)

Two Amazonas class destroyers, D10 MB *Acre* (top left) and D15 MB *Araguarí* (top right). Two Fletcher class destroyers, D27 MB *Pará* (bottom left) and D29 MB *Paraná* (bottom right). (*Marinha do Brasil*)

Two Cannon-Bertioga class destroyer escorts, D19 MB *Beberibe* (left) and D22 MB *Bocaína* (right). (*Marinha do Brasil*)

Two Imperial Marinheiro class corvettes, V15 MB *Imperial Marinheiro* (left) and V24 MB *Solimões* (right). (*Marinha do Brasil*)

Schültze class minesweeper M15 MB *Aratú* (left) and Cape/Piratini class coastal patrol boat P14 MB *Penedo*. (*Marinha do Brasil*)

(Soltam K6, M29) and guns, assault rifles (FN FAL), carbines, machine guns (FN MAG), heavy machine guns (Browning M2) and pistols (Taurus). In 1971, an elite commando group was created, the Marine Corps Special Operations Battalion (*Batalhão de Operações Especiais de Fuzileiros Navais*, COMANF).

Brazilian Naval Aviation (*Aviação Naval Brasileira*, AvN)

The Brazilian Naval Aviation was created in 1916. In 1941, with the creation of the FAB, all Naval Aviation aircraft, flight and maintenance personnel became part of the FAB. In 1952, the Navy created its Aeronautics Directorate, acquiring the light aircraft carrier *Minas Gerais* in 1956 and investing heavily in a fleet of helicopters and planes and in a new cadre of aviators. In this second phase, the issue of onboard aviation generated a serious conflict between the Navy and the FAB, which wanted a monopoly on military aviation. However, in 1965, President Castelo Branco issued a new decree, prohibiting the Navy from operating fixed-wing aircraft but authorising rotary-wing aircraft (helicopters). A third phase thus began, with the FAB embarking its planes on board the aircraft carrier *Minas Gerais* and the Navy developing its operations exclusively with helicopters.

The Brazilian Naval Aviation, was composed of a Navy Aeronautics Directorate (DAerM) and a Naval Air Force Command (ComForAerNav). In the operational sphere, the Naval Aviation had the São Pedro da Aldeia Naval Air Base (BAeNSPA) and the Aeronaval Instruction and Training Centre (CIAAN). There were four operational squadrons:

- 1st Helicopter Training Squadron (HI-1), with the the Hughes 269A/A1/B, which was later replaced by the Bell 206B Jet Ranger.

Two River patrol boats, the Pedro Teixeira class P21 MB *Raposo Tavares*, with a Helibrás HB350 Esquilo on its helicopter deck (left), and the Roraima class P32 MB *Rondônia*. (*Marinha do Brasil*)

Three Brazilian Navy submarine types: Balao/Guppy II class S12 MB *Bahía* (top left), Gatoclass S14 MB *Humaitá* (top right) and Oberon class S22 MB *Riachuelo* (bottom). (*Marinha do Brasil*)

A FAB Grumman S-2F Tracker of 1° GAE Squadron being attached to a catapult to be launched from the aircraft carrier A11 MB *Minas Gerais*. (FAB)

Marine Corps Amphibious Division Artillery Group (left). Marine Corps conscripts (right). (*Corpo de Fuzileiros Navais*)

A Naval Aviation Hughes 269 (left) and Bell 206B Jet Ranger (right). (*Marinha do Brasil,* and Carlos Morillo Doria)

Naval Aviation helicopters (clockwise from top left): Westland WS-55 Whirlwind Series 3 with a Fairchild Hiller FH-1100 in the background, Sikorsky S-61D-4 Sea King, Westland Wasp Series 3 and Sikorsky SH-34J. (*Marinha do Brasil*)

A Grumman S-2 Tracker warming up its engines while an S-61D-4 Sea King takes off from the flight deck of the aircraft carrier A11 MB *Minas Gerais*. (*Marinha do Brasil*)

- 1st General Purpose Helicopter Squadron (HU-1), with the Westland WS 51/3-2 Widgeon, Westland WS-55 Whirlwind Series 1/3, Sikorsky S-55C, Fairchild Hiller FH-1100 and Westland Wasp Series 3. All of these were later replaced by the Bell 206B Jet Ranger and Helibrás HB350B/BA Esquilo.
- 1st Anti-Submarine Helicopter Squadron (HS-1), with the Sikorsky SH-34J and later the Sikorsky S-61D, Agusta-Sikorsky ASH-3D and Sikorsky SH-3D Sea Kings.
- 1st Attack Helicopter Squadron (HA-1), with the Westland Sea Lynx HAS Mk.21 and Westland Super Lynx Mk.21A.

From 1979 onwards, district resources expanded Naval Aviation away from Rio de Janeiro. The change in the Navy's priorities and the retirement of the FAB's 1st Embarked Aviation Group (*Grupo de Aviação Embarcada*, GAE) culminated in a fourth phase. In 1998, a new decree allowed the Navy to operate fixed-wing aircraft, authorising the purchase of A-4 Skyhawk attack jets to establish the 1st Intercept and Attack Squadron (VF-1). Faced with the imminent retirement of A-11 *Minas Gerais*, a new aircraft carrier was purchased, the A-12 *São Paulo*.

A list of Brazilian Naval Aviation aircraft in service between 1964–1985 is given in Table 9.[9]

TABLE 9: Brazilian Naval Aviation Aircraft 1964–1985[10]			
Aircraft type	**Years in service**	**No. of aircraft**	**Role**
Westland WS-S1/S2 Widgeon	1958–1968	2	Utility helicopter
Bell 47J	1958–1974	3	Trainer/Utility helicopter
Kawasaki-Bell 47G-3	1958–1970	2	Trainer/Utility helicopter
Grumman TBM-3E Avenger*	1960–1965	3	Trainer
Westland WS-55 Whirlwind Series 1	1960–1968	5	Transport/SAR
Bell 47D-1	1961–1968	6	Trainer/Utility helicopter
Taylorcraft BC-12D*	1962–1965	1	Trainer/Light transport
CAP-4 Paulistinha*	1962–1965	2	Trainer/Light transport
Fairchild PT-26*	1962–1965	1	Primary trainer
North American T-28R-1/T-28A Trojan*	1963–1965	6/12	Advanced trainer/attack
Pilatus P-3.04*	1963–1965	6	Trainer/Liaison
Hughes 269A/269A-1/269B	1963–1974	6/13/1	Trainer
Sikorsky S-55C	1964	1	Transport/Utility helicopter
Sikorsky SH-34J⁺	1965–1974	6	ASW/Utility helicopter
Westland Wasp Series 3	1966–1991	11	Utility helicopter
Westland WS-55 Whirlwind Series 3	1966–1980	7	Transport/SAR
Fairchild Hiller FH-1100#	1968–1977	6	Utility helicopter
Sikorsky S-61D-4 Sea King	1970–present	6	ASW/SAR/Utility helicopter
Sikorsky SH-3D Sea King	1984–present	6	ASW/SAR/Utility helicopter
Agusta-Sikorsky ASH-3D Sea King	1969–present	4	ASW/SAR/Utility helicopter
Bell 206B Jet Ranger II	1974–1986	18	Trainer/Utility helicopter
Westland Sea Lynx HAS Mk.21	1978–present	9	ASW/attack
Westland Super Lynx Mk.21A	1978–present	9	ASW/attack
Helibrás HB350B/BA Esquilo	1979–present	21	Attack/Utility helicopter

* Aircraft transferred to the FAB in 1965
⁺ Received from the FAB in 1965
\# Four FH-1100s were transferred to the Rio de Janeiro Civil Police in 1977

Police Forces (*Forças policiais*)

In Brazil, the Federal Constitution established several different institutions for law enforcement, with public security in the hands of the Federal Police, Federal Highway Police, Federal Railway Police, Military Police and Civil Police.

The Federal Police (Polícia Federal, PF) was an institution, subordinated to the Ministry of Justice and Public Security, which exclusively exercised police functions. The headquarters were located in Brasília DF, with decentralised units in all the capitals of the states of the federation, as well as police stations and outposts in several cities across the country. The highest authority was the General Director. During the military regimes, this position was given to Army officers, as shown in Table 10.[11]

TABLE 10: Federal Police General Directors 1964–1985	
General Director	**Years**
Lieutenant Colonel Antônio Barbosa de Paula Serra	02 April 1964 to 21 June 1964
Brigadier General Riograndino Kruel	21 June 1964 to 26 August 1966
Lieutenant Colonel Newton Cypriano de Castro Leitão	26 August 1966 to 15 March 1967
Colonel Florimar Campello	15 March 1967 to 24 April 1968
Brigadier General José Bretas Cupertino	24 April 1968 to 31 October 1969
Brigadier General Walter Pires de C. e Albuquerque	31 October 1969 to 26 April 1971
Brigadier General Nilo Caneppa	26 April 1971 to 10 May 1973
Brigadier General Antônio Bandeira	10 May 1973 to 14 February 1974
Moacyr Coelho	14 February 1974 to 22 March 1985

Federal Police officers seen during the 1980s. (Polícia Federal)

Personnel of the Federal Highway Police in the 1970s (left). Some of the vehicles used as patrol cars: VW Beetle, Willys Jeep, Dodge M37 and Chevrolet C10 pick-up (right). (*Polícia Rodoviária Federal*)

The Federal Railway Police was in charge of controlling railways and trains throughout the country. (*Polícia Ferroviária Federal*)

The Federal Port Guard was in charge of security in the country's ports. (*Guarda Portuária Federal*)

The PF had a National Police Academy and several Directorates: Executive, Organised Crime, Technical-Scientific, Intelligence and Tactical Operations. There were also specialised police groups in charge of maritime affairs, bombs and explosives and Interpol. The PF agents were equipped with pistols, SMGs, MGs, shotguns, assault rifles and tear gas grenades. They also had jeeps, armoured vehicles, trucks and patrol cars.

Federal Highway Police (*Polícia Rodoviária Federal*, PRF) was part of the Federal Police subordinated to the Ministry of Justice, whose main function was to combat crimes on Brazil's highways and federal roads, as well as monitor and inspect vehicle traffic. In the 1960s and 1970s, they had a variety of vehicles to patrol the roads, such as the VW Beetle, VW Brasília, Willys Jeep, Dodge M37, Chevrolet C10 pick-up and various motorcycles. The Federal Railway Police (*Polícia Ferroviária Federal*, PFF) was created ostensibly for the patrolling of federal railways.

The Federal Port Guard (*Guarda Portuária Federal*, GPF) was subordinated to the Secretariat of Port Policies of the Ministry of Transport, Ports and Civil Aviation, whose main function was to guarantee security in federal ports. Thus, it combated the varied forms of crimes in Brazil's federal ports and also monitored, inspected and controlled the transit of vehicles, goods and people.

The Military Police (*Polícia Militar*, PM) had a structure similar to the Army, with the same ranks, and their officers and troops were auxiliary and reserve forces of the Brazilian Army in case of need. Its primary function was the preservation of public order in the Brazilian states and the Federal Districts. The Military Police were subordinated, together with the state Civil Police, to the governors of the states and Federal Districts. Each state's Military Police was commanded by a senior officer with the rank of colonel, called the General Commander. In 1967, the General Inspectorate of Military Police (IGPM) was created, subordinated to the Army. The Army carried out a national standardisation of the formation, training, career and armament of the Military Police and employed it for the purposes of the national security doctrine. The Military Police also has its own Military Fire Corps (*Corpos de Bombeiros Militares*, CBM).

The Civil Police (*Polícia Civil*, PC) is the oldest police force in Brazil. It was established in 1808 in Rio de Janeiro and was later implemented in all Brazilian states. It was headed by General Police Delegates or Chiefs of Police, who in turn command the Police Delegates. The latter were the commanders of each unit in a police station or district and were responsible for preserving public order and the safety of people and property, to act as the judicial police, launching criminal investigations aimed at tackling the practice of criminal offenses and its authorship. In 1977, the Police Aviation (*Aviação Policial*) was created in Rio de Janeiro, whose first fleet was composed of four Fairchild Hiller FH.1100 helicopters donated by Naval Aviation.

In addition, the Brazilian armed forces have their own police forces. The Army Police (*Polícia do Exército*, PE) was made up of infantry units responsible for ensuring respect for the law, orders, as well as compliance with military regulations. The Air Force Police (*Polícia da Aeronáutica*, PA) was part of the Special Air Force Infantry Battalions (BINFAE) and had the same responsibilities as the Army Police within the scope of the Brazilian Air Force. The Naval Battalion Police (*Polícia do Batalhão Naval*) perform the same duties as the Army and Air Force police organisations within the scope of the Navy.

The Military Police had servicemen and women in its ranks (above). The Military Police Academy (below left) and members of the Special Operations Command (COE) of the Military Police (below right). (*Polícia Militar*)

During the military regimes, the Military Police was used to control public demonstrations in the cities (above). Military Police VW Beetle patrol cars (below left) and a VW van (below right). (*Polícia Militar*)

Capture of criminals in an operation of the Rio de Janeiro Civil Police, with a Chevrolet Opala patrol car and a Fairchild Hiller FH-1100 helicopter behind (above left). An FH-1100 helicopter of the Rio de Janeiro Civil Police (top right). São Paulo Civil Police patrol cars: Chevrolet C10, VW Variant, VW Beetle and Dodge Dart (bottom left), and a São Paulo Civil Police operation (bottom right). (*Polícia Civil*)

Colonel José Ney Fernandes Antunes, Commander of the Army Police, in the barracks headquarters of Rio de Janeiro's DOI-CODI. The PE were armed with M3 submachine guns. (*Exército Brasileiro*)

Personnel of the Aeronautical Police of the Brazilian Air Force. (*Polícia da Aeronáutica*)

Police personnel from the Naval Battalion. (*Polícia do Batalhão Naval*)

APPENDICES

APPENDIX I: Organisation of the Brazilian Army

TABLE 12: I Exército (First Army)[1]

Unit	Location
Headquarters	Rio de Janeiro
1st Army Police Battalion	Andaraí
Guards Battalion	São Cristóvão
1st Guards Cavalry Regiment	São Cristóvão
1st Hunter Battalion	Petrópolis
3rd Hunter Battalion	Vila Velha
1st Group of 40mm Anti-Aircraft Automatic Cannons	São Cristóvão
1st MILITARY REGION (Rio de Janeiro)	Ilha do Bom Jesus
3rd Guards Company	Valença
4th Group of 90mm Anti-Aircraft Guns	Tairetá
Ammunition Depot Battalion	Deodoro
Heavy Armament Maintenance Battalion	Copacabana
Coast Artillery of the 1st Military Region	Niterói
- 1st Coast Artillery Group	Urca
- 2nd Coast Artillery Group	Copacabana
- 3rd Coast Artillery Group	Gávea
- 8th Mobile Coast Artillery Group	São Gonçalo
- 1st Railway Coast Artillery Group	Morro do Pico
- 1st Coastal Howitzer Battery	Leme
- 2nd Coastal Howitzer Battery	Macaé
- 1st Battery of the 10th Mobile Coast Artillery Group	Imbuí
- 1st Battery of the 1st Mobile Coast Artillery Group	Lage
- 1st Battery of the 4th Coast Artillery Group	Vila Militar
1st Infantry Division	Vila Militar
- 1st Army Police Company	Vila Militar
- 1st Mechanized Reconnaissance Squadron	
- 1st Combat Engineering Battalion)	Santa Cruz
- 1st Health Battalion	Rio de Janeiro
- Divisional Infantry of the 1st Infantry Division	Vila Militar
1st Infantry Regiment: 1st and 2nd Battalions	Vila Militar
2nd Infantry Regiment: 1st and 2nd Battalions	Vila Militar
3rd Battalion	Suez, Egypt (UN)
3rd Infantry Regiment: 1st and 2nd Battalions	São Gonçalo
- Divisional Artillery of the 1st Infantry Division	Vila Militar
1st 105mm Howitzer Regiment: First and Second Groups	Vila Militar
1st Group of 155mm Howitzers	Deodoro
- Group of School Units	Vila Militar
Infantry School Regiment: 1st, 2nd and 3rd Battalions	Vila Militar
Cavalry School Regiment	Vila Militar
Artillery School Regiment: First Group	Vila Militar
Engineering School Battalion	Vila Militar
1st Group of 90mm Anti-Aircraft Cannons	Deodoro
Maintenance School Battalion	Vila Militar
Mechanized Reconnaissance School Squadron	Deodoro
- Airborne Division Centre	Deodoro
Airborne Infantry Battalion	Deodoro
Airborne Howitzer Group	Deodoro
1st Airborne Engineering Company	Deodoro
- Armoured Division	Rio de Janeiro
1st Tank Battalion	Avenida Brasil
2nd Tank Battalion	Deodoro
3rd Tank Battalion	Raelengo
1st Armoured Infantry Battalion	Barra Mansa
2nd Armoured Infantry Battalion	São Cristóvão
1st Mechanized Reconnaissance Regiment Maintenance Battalion	Campinho
Maintenance Battalion	São Cristóvão

4th MILITARY REGION (Juiz de Fora)	
4th Infantry Division	Juiz de Fora
4th Combat Engineering Battalion	Itajubá
4th Army Police Company	Juiz de Fora
4th Mechanized Reconnaissance Squadron	Juiz de Fora
Divisional Infantry of the 4th Infantry Division	Belo Horizonte
- 10th Infantry Regiment: 1st Battalion	Juiz de Fora
- 11th Infantry Regiment: 1st Battalion	São João Del-Rei
- 12th Infantry Regiment: 1st and 2nd Battalions	Belo Horizonte
- Divisional Artillery of the 4th Infantry Division	Pouso Alegre
- 4th 105mm Howitzer Regiment	Pouso Alegre
First Group	Juiz de Fora
Second Group	Pouso Alegre

TABLE 13: II Exército (Second Army)[2]

Military Unit	City
Headquarters	São Paulo
2nd Hunter Battalion	São Vicente
4th Hunter Battalion	Lins
1st Battalion of Light Tanks	Campinas
17th Mechanized Cavalry Regiment	Pirassununga
2nd MILITARY REGION (São Paulo)	
7th Guards Company	São Paulo
Coastal and Anti-Aircraft Artillery of the 2nd Military Region	Santos
- 3rd Coastal Howitzer Battery	Monduba
- 5th Coastal Artillery Group	Praia Grande
- 6th Mobile Coastal Artillery Group	Santos
- 2nd Group of 90mm Anti-Aircraft Cannons	Quitaúna
- 5th Group of 90mm Anti-Aircraft Cannons	Campinas
- 2nd Group of 40mm Anti-Aircraft Automatic Cannons	Barueri
- 5th Group of 40mm Anti-Aircraft Automatic Cannons	Santos
2nd Infantry Division	São Paulo
- 2nd Army Police Company	São Paulo
- 2nd Combat Engineering Battalion	Pindamonhangaba
- 2nd Health Battalion	São Paulo
- 2nd Mechanized Reconnaissance Squadron	São Paulo
- Divisional Infantry of the 2nd Infantry Division	Caçapava
- 4th Infantry Regiment: 1st and 2nd Battalions	Quitaúna
- 5th Infantry Regiment: 1st Battalion	Lorena
- 6th Infantry Regiment: 1st Battalion	Caçapava
- Divisional Artillery of the 2nd Infantry Division	Jundiaí
2nd 105mm Howitzer Regiment: First Group	Itu
2nd Group of 155mm Howitzers	Jundiaí
9th MILITARY REGION (Campo Grande)	
4th Cavalry Division	Campo Grande
- 14th Army Police Company	Campo Grande
- 10th Mechanized Cavalry Regiment	Bela Vista
- 11th Mechanized Cavalry Regiment	Ponta Porã
- 1st Squadron of the 4th Motorized Cavalry Regiment	Três Lagoas
- 1st Squadron of the 4th Mechanized Reconnaissance Regiment	Campo Grande
- 9th Self-propelled 75mm Cannon Group	Nioaque
- 10th Group of 75mm Self-propelled Cannons	Campo Grande
- 1st Company of the 9th Combat Engineering Battalion	Aquidauana
2nd Mixed Brigade	Corumbá
- 16th Hunter Battalion	Cuiabá
- 17th Hunter Battalion	Corumbá
- 2nd Border Battalion	Cáceres
- 2nd Border Company	Porto Murtinho
- 1st Battery of the 6th Coast Artillery Group	Coimbra

TABLE 14: III Exército (Third Army)[3]	
Military Unit	**City**
Headquarters	Porto Alegre
1st Railway Battalion	Bento Gonçalves
2nd Railway Battalion	Rio Negro
2nd Road Battalion	Lages
3rd Road Battalion	Vacaria
3rd MILITARY REGION (Porto Alegre)	
1st Guards Company	Porto Alegre
2nd Battalion of Light Tanks	Santo Ângelo
3rd Battalion of Light Tanks	Santa María
3rd Group of 40mm Anti-Aircraft Automatic Cannons	Caxias do Sul
7th Mobile Coastal Artillery Group	Rio Grande
3rd Infantry Division	Santa María
- 3rd Combat Engineering Battalion	Cachoeira do Sul
- 3rd Mechanized Reconnaissance Squadron	Santa María
- Divisional Infantry of the 3rd Infantry Division	Pelotas
7th Infantry Regiment: 1st and 2nd Battalions	Santa María
8th Infantry Regiment: 1st Battalion	Santa Cruz do Sul
9th Infantry Regiment: 1st and 2nd Battalions	Pelotas
- Divisional Artillery of the 3rd Infantry Division	Santa María
3rd Self-propelled 75mm Artillery Regiment: First Group	Santa Maria
1st Group of the 3rd 105mm Howitzer Regiment	Cachoeira do Sul
6th Infantry Division	Porto Alegre
- 6th Army Police Company	Porto Alegre
- 6th Combat Engineering Battalion	Porto Alegre
- 6th Mechanized Reconnaissance Squadron	Porto Alegre
- Divisional Infantry of the 6th Infantry Division	São Leopoldo
17th Infantry Regiment: 1st and 2nd Battalions	Cruz Alta
18th Infantry Regiment: 1st and 2nd Battalions	Porto Alegre
19th Infantry Regiment: 1st and 2nd Battalions	São Leopoldo
- Divisional Artillery of the 6th Infantry Division	Cruz Alta
6th Self-propelled 75mm Artillery Regiment: First Group	Cruz Alta
1st Group of the 6th 105mm Howitzer Regiment	São Leopoldo
1st Cavalry Division	Santiago
- 1st Cavalry Regiment	Itaqui
- 2nd Cavalry Regiment	São Borja
- 3rd Cavalry Regiment	São Luiz Gonzaga
- 4th Cavalry Regiment	Santiago
- 1st Squadron of the 20th Cavalry Regiment	Passo Fundo
- 1st Mechanized Reconnaissance Regiment	Santo Ângelo
- 1st Motorized Cavalry Regiment	Santa Rosa
1st 75mm Artillery Group on Horseback	São Borja
- 2nd 75mm Artillery Group on Horseback	Santiago
- 7th Group of 75mm Self-propelled Cannons	Ijuí
2nd Cavalry Division	Uruguaiana
- 5th Cavalry Regiment	Quaraí
- 6th Cavalry Regiment	Alegrete
- 7th Cavalry Regiment	Livramento
- 8th Cavalry Regiment	Uruguaiana
- 2nd Mechanized Reconnaissance Regiment	Porto Alegre
- 2nd Motorized Cavalry Regiment	Rosário do Sul
- 4th 75mm Artillery Group on Horseback	Uruguaiana
- 8th 75 mm Artillery Group on Horseback	Livramento
- 3rd Group of 75mm Self-propelled Cannons	Alegrete
- 12th Combat Engineering Battalion	Alegrete
3rd Cavalry Division	Bagé
- 9th Cavalry Regiment	São Gabriel
- 12th Cavalry Regiment	Bagé
- 13th Cavalry Regiment	Jaguarão
- 14th Cavalry Regiment	Dom Pedrito
- 3rd Mechanized Reconnaissance Regiment	Bagé
- 3rd Motorized Cavalry Regiment	São Gabriel
- 3rd 75mm Artillery Regiment on Horseback: First and Second Groups	Bagé

Military Unit	City
5th MILITARY REGION (Curitiba)	
13th Hunter Battalion	Joinville
14th Hunter Battalion	Florianópolis
1st Border Battalion	Foz do Iguaçu
5th Border Company	Guaíra
1st Cavalry Independent Squadron	Guarapuava
2nd Cavalry Independent Squadron	Palmas
1st Battery of the 5th Mobile Coast Artillery Group	São Francisco
3rd 75mm Artillery Group	Castro
5th Infantry Division	Curitiba
- 5th Army Police Company	Curitiba
- 5th Combat Engineering Battalion	Porto União
- 5th Mechanized Reconnaissance Squadron	Curitiba
- Divisional Infantry of the 5th Infantry Division	Ponta Grossa
1st Company of the 13th Infantry Regiment	Francisco Beltrão
13th Infantry Regiment: 1st and 2nd Battalions	Ponta Grossa
20th Infantry Regiment: 1st Battalion	Curitiba
23rd Infantry Regiment: 1st Battalion	Blumenau
- Divisional Artillery of the 5th Infantry Division	Curitiba
5th 105mm Howitzer Regiment: First and Second Group	Curitiba
	Lapa & Curitiba

TABLE 15: IV Exército (Fourth Army)[4]

Military Unit	City
Headquarters	Recife
1st Construction Engineering Battalion	Caicó
2nd Construction Engineering Battalion	Teresina
3rd Construction Engineering Battalion	Natal
4th Construction Engineering Battalion	Crateús
6th MILITARY REGION (Salvador)	
4th Guards Company	Salvador
19th Hunter Battalion	Salvador
28th Hunter Battalion	Aracaju
1st Independent Rifle Company	São Francisco Power Plant
1st Battery of the 4th Mobile Coast Artillery Group	Salvador
7th MILITARY REGION (Recife)	
2nd Guards Company	Recife
20th Hunter Battalion	Maceió
3rd Group of 88mm Anti-Aircraft Cannons	Natal
1st Battery of the 3rd Mobile Coast Artillery Group	Olinda
Fernando de Noronha Garrison	Fernando de Noronha
7th Infantry Division	Recife
- 7th Army Police Company	Recife
- 7th Mechanized Reconnaissance Squadron	Recife
- 1st Group of the 7th 105mm Howitzer Regiment	Olinda
- Divisional Infantry of the 7th Infantry Division	Natal
14th Infantry Regiment: 1st and 2nd Battalions	Jaboatão
15th Infantry Regiment: 1st Battalion	João Pessoa
16th Infantry Regiment: 1st Battalion	Natal
10th MILITARY REGION (Fortaleza)	
23rd Hunter Battalion	Fortaleza
24th Hunter Battalion	São Luís
25th Hunter Battalion	Teresina
10th Transported 75mm Artillery Group	Fortaleza

TABLE 16: Comando Militar da Amazônia (Amazónia Military Command)[5]	
Military Unit	**City**
Headquarters	Belém
8th MILITARY REGION (Belém)	
5th Guards Company	Belém
26th Hunter Battalion	
1st Company of the 3rd Border Battalion	Belém
Border Element Group	Clevelândia
- 27th Hunter Battalion	Manáus
- 3rd Border Company	Manáus
- 4th Border Company	Porto Velho
- 6th Border Company	Rio Branco
- 7th Border Company	Guarajá
- 8th Border Company	Tabatinga
- 1st Border Platoon	Cruzeiro do Sul
- 2nd Border Platoon	Boa Vista
- 3rd Border Platoon	Ipiranga
- 4th Border Platoon	Japurá
- 7th Border Platoon	Cucuí
- 8th Border Platoon	Príncipe da Beira
- 9th Border Platoon	Palmeiras
- 10th Border Platoon	Estirão do Equador
- 11th Border Platoon	Brasileia
	Thaumaturgo

TABLE 17: Comando Militar de Brasília (Brasília Military Command)[6]	
Military Unit	**City**
Headquarters	Brasília DF
11th MILITARY REGION (Brasília DF)	
Army Police Company of the 11th Military Region	Brasília DF
Presidential Guard Battalion	Brasília DF
6th Hunter Battalion	Ipameri
10th Hunter Battalion	Goiânia
1st Independent Anti-Aircraft Automatic Cannon Battery	Brasília DF

APPENDIX II: Brazilian Air Force Aircraft Types

TABLE 18: Brazilian Air Force Aircraft Types in Service 1963–1985[7]		
Aircraft Type/Years in service	**Number of aircraft***	**Role**
Gloster G-41K Meteor FMk.8 (1953–1974)	61	Fighter
Gloster G-43 Meteor TMk.7 (1953–1971)	10	Advanced trainer
Lockheed TF-33A/AT-33A T-Bird (1956–1975)	58	Advanced trainer/attack
Lockheed F-80C Shooting Star (1958–1973)	33	Tactical fighter
Embraer EMB-326/AT-26 Xavante (1971–2014)	166	Advanced trainer/attack
Embraer EMB-327/AT-27 Tucano (1983–present)	136	Advanced trainer/attack
Dassault Mirage III EBR (1972–2005)	17	Fighter/Interceptor
Dassault Mirage III DBR (1972–2005)	6	Advanced trainer
Northrop F-5E Tiger II (1975–present)	36	Tactical fighter
Northrop F-5B (1975–1996)	6	Advanced trainer
Cessna T-37C Tweety Bird (1967–1981)	65	Advanced trainer
Aérospatiale/Fouga CM.170 Super Magister (1969–1974)	7	Air Demonstration Squadron+

North American B-25B/C/D/J Mitchel (1942–1974)	87	Medium bomber/transport
Douglas A-20K (1944–1968)	31	Medium bomber/attack
Boeing B-17G (1951–1969)	12	SAR/Reconnaissance
Douglas A/B-26B/C Invader (1957–1975)	14/18	Medium bomber/attack
Lockheed P2V-5 Neptune (1959–1976)	14	ASW/Maritime reconnaissance
Grumman S-2A/E Tracker (1961–1996)	13/14	ASW/Maritime reconnaissance
Fokker S.11/T-21 (1956–1973)	100	Primary trainer
Fokker S.12/T-22 (1960–1973)	49	Primary trainer
Neiva T-25 Universal (1968–present)	150	Trainer
Aerotec A-122A T-23 Uirapurú (1969–1984)	76	Primary trainer
Morane Saulnier MS-760 Paris (1959–1974)	30	Advanced trainer/Liaison
North American T-6B/C/D/G/SNJ-5C/SNJ-6C (1942–1976)	427	Advanced trainer/attack
North American T-28A/R1 Trojan (1965–1972)	12/5	Advanced trainer
Pilatus P.3-04 (1965–1972)	5	Trainer
Lockheed 18 Lodestar (1941–1968)	9	Transport
Beechcraft C-18S/T-7 Navigator (1942–1976)	42	Navigation trainer/transport
Beechcraft AT-11 (1943–1975)	22	Bomber trainer/Air photography
Beechcraft D-18S (1946–1976)	28	Transport
Beechcraft E-18S (1957–1976)	7	Transport
Beechcraft H-18S (1964–1977)	16	Transport/trainer
Consolidated Vultee PBY-5/5A/6 Catalina (1943–1982)	31	ASW/transport
Douglas C-47A/B (1944–1983)	89	Transport
Curtiss C-46 Commando (1948–1968)	2	Transport
Douglas C-54G Skymaster (1960–1968)	12	Transport
Vickers V.742D/V.789D Viscount (1957–1987)	1/1	Presidential/VIP transport
Douglas DC-6B/C-118 Liftmaster (1968–1975)	5	Transport
Lockheed C-130E/H/KC-130H (1965–present)	11/16/2	Heavy transport/air refuelling
BAC 1-11 (1968–1976)	2	Presidential transport
Boeing 737-2N3 (1976–2010)	2	Presidential transport
De Havilland Canada DHC-5A Buffalo (1968–2011)	24	Troop/freight transport
Grumman SA-16A Albatross (1958–1980)	14	SAR
Fairchild C-82A Packet (1956–1968)	12	Troop/freight transport
Fairchild C-119G Flying Boxcar (1962–1975)	13	Troop/freight transport
Avro 748 Series 2/2A (1962–2006)	6/6	Transport
Hawker Siddeley HS-125 (1968–2010)	15	VIP transport/radio aid calibration
Cessna 305A/E/O-1 Bird Dog (1957–1980)	9/11	Liaison/FAC
Cessna 180B (1959–1972)	1	Liaison
Cessna 185A (1966–1979)	1	Light transport
Neiva 56B/D Paulistinha (1959–1974)	208	Liaison
Neiva 591/592 U42 Regente ELO (1965–2011)	80/41	Light transport/FAC
Beechcraft 55 Baron (1966–1989)	1	Light transport
Beechcraft 65 Queen Air (1969–1977)	2	Light transport

Piper PA-23-250 Aztec (1966–1986)	1	Light transport
Embraer EMB-110A Bandeirante (1973–2014)	62	Transport/trainer/radio air calibration
Embraer EMB-110K1/P1/M (1977–present)	68/38	Transport/trainer/radio air calibration
Embraer EMB-111 Bandeirulha (1978–2014)	12	ASW/Maritime reconnaissance
Embraer EMB-810 Seneca II/IIA (1977–2010)	35	Light transport
Embraer EMB-121A Xingú (1978–2010)	7	VIP transport
Embraer EMB-201R Ipanema (1976–2011)	3	Glider trailer#
Bell 47D1 (1953–1968)	3	Utility helicopter
Bell 47J (1958–1974)	5	Utility helicopter
Bell 47G2/OH-13H (1959–1990)	12/36	Trainer/Liaison
Sikorsky S-55 (1958–1969)	4	SAR/Utility helicopter
Sikorsky SH-34J (1961–1965)	6	ASW/transport
Bell UH-1D (1967–present)	14	Troop transport/SAR/attack
Bell UH-1H (1972–present)	54	Troop transport/SAR/attack
Bell 206A Jet Ranger (1969–1989)	7	VIP transport/utility helicopter
Aérospatiale SA-330L Puma (1981–1986)	6	Tactical support/transport
Blanik L-13J (1976-2006)	10	Glider#
Glasflügel Standard Libelle 201B (1979–present)	1	Glider#
Ipe KW-1b2 Quero-Quero II (1980–2001)	16	Glider trainer#
Ipe 02b Nhapecan II (1980–2001)	15	Glider trainer#
Schleicher ASW-20 (1981–present)	1	High performance glider#
Quicksilver MX/MXL II (1984–1996)	14/6	Ultralight aircraft#

* Total of aircraft used by the FAB
\+ Used by the Esquadrilha da Fumaça (Smoke Squadron) air display team
\# Air Force Academy (AFA) Flight Club

TABLE 19: Brazilian Air Force Aircraft Designations[8]

Aircraft type	FAB designation
Gloster G-41K Meteor FMk 8	F-8
Gloster G-43 Meteor TMk.7	TF-7
Lockheed T-33A/AT-33A T-Bird	TF-33 & AT-33A
Lockheed F-80C Shooting Star	F-80C
Embraer EMB-326 Xavante	AT-26
Embraer EMB-327 Tucano	T-27, AT-27 & A-27
Dassault Mirage III EBR	F-103E
Dassault Mirage III DBR	F-103D
Northrop F-5E Tiger II	F-5E
Northrop F-5B	F-5B
Cessna T-37C Tweety Bird	T-37C
North American B-25B/C/D/J Mitchel	B-25, B-25J, RB-25J & CB-25
Douglas A-20K	A-20K, A-20C & R-20
Boeing B-17G	B-17G
Douglas A/B-26B/C Invader	A-26B, B-26B, A-26C, B-26C & CB-26

Lockheed P2V-5 Neptune	P-15
Grumman S-2A/E Tracker	P-16, P-16A, P-16E, UP-16A & P-16H
Fokker S.11	T-21
Fokker S.12	T-22
Aerotec A-122A Uirapurú	T-23
Aérospatiale/Fouga CM.170 Super Magister	T-24
Neiva T-25 Universal	T-25, T-25A, T-25C & AT-25
Morane Saulnier MS-760 Paris	C-41
North American T-6B/C/D/G/SNJ-5C/SNJ-6C	T-6B, T-6C, T-6D, T-6G & T-6-SNJ-5C/6C
North American T-28A/R1 Trojan	T-28R
Pilatus P.3-04	L-3 & O-3
Lockheed 18 Lodestar	C-60A & VC-60
Beechcraft C-18S/T-7 Navigator	AT-7, T-7 & UT-7
Beechcraft AT-11	AT-11, T-11 & RT-11
Beechcraft D-18S	UC-45F, C-45 & U-45
Beechcraft E-18S	E-18S, C-45, VC-45 & U-45
Beechcraft H-18S	TC-45T, U-45T, C-45T & VC-45T
Consolidated Vultee PBY-5/5A/6 Catalina	PA-10, CA-10, CA-10A & C-10
Douglas C-47A/B	C-47, C-47A, EC-47 & VC-47
Curtiss C-46 Commando	C-46
Douglas C-54G Skymaster	C-54G
Vickers V.742D/V.789D Viscount	VC-90 & C-90
Douglas DC-6B Liftmaster	C-118
Lockheed C-130E/H/KC-130H	C-130, SC-130 & KC-130
BAC 1-11	VC-92
Boeing 737-2N3	VC-96
De Havilland Canada DHC-5A Buffalo	C-115
Grumman SA-16A Albatross	U-16, M-16, SA-16 & SA-16A
Fairchild C-82A Packet	C-82A
Fairchild C-119G Flying Boxcar	C-119G
Avro 748 Series 2/2A	C-91 & C-91A
Hawker Siddeley HS-125	VC-93, EC-93, VU-93, EU-93 & XU-93
Cessna 305A/E Bird Dog	L-19A, L-19E, O-19A & O-19E
Cessna 180B	L-19
Cessna 185A	U-37
Neiva 56B/D Paulistinha	L-6 & O-6
Neiva 591/592 U42 Regente ELO	C-42 & L-42
Beechcraft 55 Baron	C-55
Beechcraft 65 Queen Air	C-8 & EU-8
Piper PA-23-250 Aztec	U-36
Embraer EMB-110A Bandeirante	C-95 & EC-95A
Embraer EMB-110K1/P1/M	C-95A, C-95B, C-95C, IC-95B, EC-95C, IC-95C & SC-95B

Embraer EMB-111 Bandeirulha	P-95, P-95A & P-95B
Embraer EMB-810 Seneca II/IIA	U-7, U-7A & U-7B
Embraer EMB-121A Xingú	VU-9
Embraer EMB-201R Ipanema	U-19 & G-19
Bell 47D1	H-13D
Bell 47J	H-13J
Bell 47G2	H-13H & OH-13H
Sikorsky S-55	H-19D & SH-19
Sikorsky SH-34J	H-34
Bell 205A	SH-1D & UH-1D
Bell 205A-1	UH-1H & H-1H
Bell 206A Jet Ranger	H-4
Aérospatiale SA-330L Puma	CH-33
Blanik L-13J	TZ-13
Glasflügel Standard Libelle 201B	Z-15
Ipe KW-1b2 Quero-Quero II	Z-16
Ipe 02b Nhapecan II	TZ-14
Schleicher ASW-20	Z-20
Quicksilver MX/MXL II	T-8A & T-8B
F= fighter, TF= fighter trainer, B= bomber, A= attack, AT= attack trainer, T= trainer, P= maritime reconnaissance, C= cargo, H=helicopter, VC= VIP transport, O= observation, L= liaison, U= utility, E=electronic, S=search, TZ= glider trainer, Z= glider	

APPENDIX III: Brazilian Navy

TABLE 20: Brazilian Navy Ships on Strength 1964–1985[9]

Type/Class/Years in service	Pennant number	Name	Tons	Crew
Aircraft carrier (Colossus) (1956–2001) (H)	A-11	MB *Minas Geráis*	19,890	1,300
Light cruiser (Brooklyn) (1951–1973) (H)	CL-11	MB *Almirante Barroso*	9,700	868
Light cruiser (Brooklyn) (1951–1976) (H)	CL-12	MB *Marquês de Tamandaré*	13,541	888
Destroyer (Amazonas) (1945–1974)	D-10	MB *Acre*	1,418	215
Destroyer (Amazonas) (1957–1964)	D-11	MB *Ajuricaba*	1,450	230
Destroyer (Amazonas) (1949–1973)	D-12	MB *Amazonas*	1,805	240
Destroyer (Amazonas) (1949–1974)	D-14	MB *Araguaia*	1,370	220
Destroyer (Amazonas) (1951–1974)	D-15	MB *Araguari*	1,370	220
Destroyer escort (Cannon/Bertioga) (1945–1964)	D-16	MB *Babitonga*	1,240	216
Destroyer escort (Cannon/Bertioga) (1944–1973)	D-17	MB *Baependi*	1,240	216
Destroyer escort (Cannon/Bertioga) (1944–1981)	D-18	MB *Baurú*	1,240	216
Destroyer escort (Cannon/Bertioga) (1944–1968)	D-19	MB *Beberibe*	1,309	216
Destroyer escort Cannon/Bertioga) (1944–1964)	D-20	MB *Benevente*	1,309	216
Destroyer escort (Cannon/Bertioga) (1944–1964)	D-21	MB *Bertioga*	1,309	216
Destroyer escort (Cannon/Bertioga) (1945–1975)	D-22	MB *Bocaina*	1,309	216
Destroyer escort (Cannon/Bertioga) (1944–1972)	D-23	MB *Bracuí*	1,309	216

Destroyer (Marcílio Dias) (1943–1965)	D-24	MB *Greenhalgh*	1,500	210
Destroyer (Marcílio Dias) (1945–1992) (H)	D-25	MB *Marcílio Dias*	2,425	301
Destroyer (Gearing) (1973–1997) (H)	D-26	MB *Mariz e Barros*	2,425	301
Destroyer (Fletcher) (1959–1978)	D-27	MB *Pará*	2,050	310
Destroyer (Fletcher) (1959–1978)	D-28	MB *Paraíba*	2,050	310
Destroyer (Fletcher) (1961–1982)	D-29	MB *Paraná*	2,050	310
Destroyer (Fletcher) (1961–1982)	D-30	MB *Pernambuco*	2,050	310
Destroyer (Fletcher) (1967–1989)	D-31	MB *Piauí*	2,050	310
Destroyer (Fletcher) (1968–1988)	D-32	MB *Santa Catarina*	2,050	310
Destroyer (Fletcher) (1972–1990)	D-33	MB *Maranhão*	2,050	310
Destroyer (Allen M. Sumner) (1972–1990)	D-34	MB *Mato Grosso*	2,200	304
Destroyer (Allen M. Sumner) (1973–1995) (H)	D-35	MB *Sergipe*	2,200	274
Destroyer (Allen M. Sumner) (1973–1995) (H)	D-36	MB *Alagoas*	2,341	287
Destroyer (Allen M. Sumner) (1973–1996) (H)	D-37	MB *Rio Grande do Norte*	2,200	274
Destroyer (Allen M. Sumner) (1973–1996) (H)	D-38	MB *Espíritu Santo*	2,200	274
Frigate (Niterói) (1976–present) (H) (M)	F-40	MB *Niterói*	3,800	200
Frigate (Niterói) (1977–present) (H) (M)	F-41	MB *Defensora*	3,800	200
Frigate (Niterói) (1978–present) (H) (M)	F-42	MB *Constituição*	3,800	200
Frigate (Niterói) (1977–present) (H) (M)	F-43	MB *Liberal*	3,800	200
Frigate (Niterói) (1979–present) (H) (M)	F-44	MB *Independência*	3,800	200
Frigate (Niterói) (1980–present) (H) (M)	F-45	MB *União*	3,800	200
Corvette (Imperial Marinheiro) (1955–present)	V-15	MB *Imperial Marinheiro*	911	64
Corvette (Imperial Marinheiro) (1955–1995)	V-16	MB *Iguatemi*	911	64
Corvette (Imperial Marinheiro) (1954–1983)	V-17	MB *Ipiranga*	911	64
Corvette (Imperial Marinheiro) (1954–1996)	V-18	MB *Forte de Coimbra*	911	64
Corvette (Imperial Marinheiro) (1955–present)	V-19	MB *Caboclo*	911	64
Corvette (Imperial Marinheiro) (1955–2004)	V-20	MB *Angostura*	911	64
Corvette (Imperial Marinheiro) (1954–2002)	V-21	MB *Bahiana*	911	64
Corvette (Imperial Marinheiro) (1954–1998)	V-22	MB *Bearim*	911	64
Corvette (Imperial Marinheiro) (1954–2002)	V-23	MB *Purus*	911	64
Corvette (Imperial Marinheiro) (1954–2003)	V-24	MB *Solimões*	911	64
Minesweeper (YSM 1) (1960–1982)	M-11	MB *Javarí*	270	33
Minesweeper (YSM 1) (1960–present)	M-12	MB *Jutaí*	270	33
Minesweeper (YSM 1) (1963–1982)	M-13	MB *Juruá*	270	33
Minesweeper (YSM 1) (1963–1974)	M-14	MB *Juruena*	270	33
Minesweeper (Schültze) (1971–present)	M-15	MB *Aratú*	241	36
Minesweeper (Schültze) (1971–present)	M-16	MB *Anhatomirim*	241	36
Minesweeper (Schültze) (1971–present)	M-17	MB *Atalaia*	241	36
Minesweeper (Schültze) (1972–present)	M-18	MB *Araçatuba*	241	36
Minesweeper (Schültze) (1975–present)	M-19	MB *Abrolhos*	241	36
Minesweeper (Schültze) (1975–present)	M-20	MB *Albardão*	241	36
Submarine hunter (Piranha) (1947–1971)	J-28	MB *Pirajú*	137	30

Submarine hunter (Piranha) (1947–1964)	J-29	MB *Pirambú*	137	30
Submarine hunter (Piranha) (1947–1971)	J-30	MB *Piranha*	137	30
Submarine hunter (Piranha) (1948–1965)	J-31	MB *Pirapiá*	137	30
Submarine hunter (Piranha) (1948–1972)	J-32	MB *Piraquê*	137	30
Submarine hunter (Piranha) (1948–1960)	J-33	MB *Piraúna*	137	30
Submarine (Balao/Guppy II) (1972–1983)	S-10	MB *Guanabara*	1,870	83
Submarine (Corsair/Guppy II) (1972–1978)	S-11	MB *Rio Grande do Sul*	1,870	83
Submarine (Balao/Guppy II) (1973–1993)	S-12	MB *Bahía*	1,870	83
Submarine (Tench/Guppy II) (1972–1978)	S-13	MB *Rio de Janeiro*	1,870	83
Submarine (Gato) (1957–1967)	S-14	MB *Humaitá*	1,475	70
Submarine (Corsair/Guppy II) (1973–1987)	S-14	MB *Ceará*	1,870	83
Submarine (Gato) (1957–1966)	S-15	MB *Riachuelo*	1,475	70
Submarine (Balao/Guppy III) (1973–1990)	S-15	MB *Goiás*	2,007	74
Submarine (Balao/Guppy III) (1973–1992)	S-16	MB *Amazonas*	1,975	83
Submarine (Oberon) (1973–1996)	S-20	MB *Humaitá*	2,030	74
Submarine (Oberon) (1977–2001)	S-21	MB *Tonelero*	2,030	74
Submarine (Oberon) (1977–1997)	S-22	MB *Riachuelo*	2,030	74
Coastal patrol ship (Cape/Piratini) (1970–present)	P-10	MB *Piratini*	105	16
Coastal patrol ship (Cape/Piratini) (1971–present)	P-11	MB *Pirajá*	105	16
Coastal patrol ship (Cape/Piratini) (1971–present)	P-12	MB *Pampeiro*	105	16
Coastal patrol ship (Cape/Piratini) (1971–present)	P-13	MB *Paratí*	105	16
Coastal patrol ship (Cape/Piratini) (1971–present)	P-14	MB *Penedo*	105	16
Coastal patrol ship (Cape/Piratini) (1971–present)	P-15	MB *Poti*	105	16
River patrol boat (Pedro Teixeira) (1973–present) (H)	P-20	MB *Pedro Teixeira*	582	80
River patrol boat (Pedro Teixeira) (1973–present) (H)	P-21	MB *Raposo Tavares*	582	80
River patrol boat (Roraima) (1975–present) (H)	P-30	MB *Roraima*	340	56
River patrol boat (Roraima) (1975–present) (H)	P-31	MB *Rondônia*	340	56
River patrol boat (Roraima) (1976–present) (H)	P-32	MB *Amapá*	340	56
Training vessel (Aspirante Nascimento)(1980–present)	U-10	MB *Aspirante Nascimento*	120	16
Training vessel (Aspirante Nascimento)(1981–present)	U-11	MB *Guarda-Marinha Jansen*	120	16
Training vessel (Aspirante Nascimento)(1981–present)	U-12	MB *Guarda-Marinha Brito*	120	16
River monitor (Parnaíba) (1938–present)	U-17	MB *Parnaíba*	620	74
Hospital ship (Oswaldo Cruz) (1984–present)	U-18	MB *Oswaldo Cruz*	360	27
Hospital ship (Oswaldo Cruz) (1984–present)	U-19	MB *Carlos Chagas*	360	27
Ocean tug (Rio Doce) (1954–present)	U-20	MB *Rio Doce*	150	10
Ocean tug (Rio Doce) (1954–present)	U-21	MB *Rio das Contas*	150	10
Ocean tug (Rio Doce) (1954–present)	U-22	MB *Rio Formoso*	150	10
Ocean tug (Rio Doce) (1955–present)	U-23	MB *Rio Real*	150	10
Ocean tug (Rio Doce) (1954–present)	U-24	MB *Rio Turvo*	150	10
Ocean tug (Rio Doce) (1954–present)	U-25	MB *Rio Verde*	150	10
Training vessel (LC-62) (1984–present)	U-31	MB *Rosca Fina*	18	16
Training vessel (LC-62) (1984–present)	U-32	MB *Voga Picada*	18	16

Training vessel (LC-62) (1984–present)	U-33	MB *Leva Arriba*	18	16
Transport ship (Pardo) (1976–present)	U-40	MB *Rio Pardo*	150	10
Transport ship (Pardo) (1976–present)	U-41	MB *Rio Negro*	150	10
Transport ship (Pardo) (1976–present)	U-42	MB *Rio Chuí*	150	10
Transport ship (Pardo) (1976–present)	U-40	MB *Rio Oiapoque*	150	10
Port tug (Comandante Marriog) (1981–present)	R-15	MB *Comandante Marriog*	115	6
Port tug (Comandante Marriog) (1981–present)	R-16	MB *Comandante Didier*	115	6
Port tug (Comandante Marriog) (1982–present)	R-17	MB *Tenente Magalhães*	115	6
Port tug (Comandante Marriog) (1982–present)	R-18	MB *Cabo Schramm*	115	6
Ocean tug (Sotoyomo) (1947–1986)	R-21	MB *Tritão*	534	45
Ocean tug (Sotoyomo) (1947–1986)	R-22	MB *Tridente*	534	45
Ocean tug (Sotoyomo) (1947–1985)	R-23	MB *Triunfo*	534	45
Ocean tug (Almirante Guilhem) (1981–present)	R-24	MB *Almirante Guilhem*	2,400	40
Ocean tug (Almirante Guilhem) (1981–present)	R-25	MB *Almirante Guillobel*	2,400	40
Tug (Audaz) (1953–1986)	R-31	MB *Audaz*	130	12
Tug (Audaz) (1953–1986)	R-32	MB *Centauro*	130	12
Tug (Audaz) (1953–1986)	R-33	MB *Guaraní*	130	12
Tug (Audaz) (1953–1986)	R-34	MB *Lamego*	130	12
Tug (Audaz) (1953–1986)	R-35	MB *Passo da Patria*	130	12
Tug (Audaz) (1953–1986)	R-36	MB *Voluntario*	130	12
River transport ship (Paraguassu) (1972–present) (H)	G-15	MB *Paraguassú*	200	35
Troop transport ship (Custódio de Mello) (1955–1995)	G-16	MB *Barroso Pereira*	5,480	160
Gasoline tanker (Mettawee) (1948–1970)	G-18	MB *Rijo*	2,200	35
Gasoline tanker (Mettawee) (1948–1970)	G-19	MB *Raza*	2,200	35
Troop transport ship (Custódio de Mello) (1955–2002)	G-20	MB *Custódio de Melo*	5,820	127
Troop transport ship (Custódio de Mello) (1957–2009)	G-21	MB *Ary Parreiras*	7,438	147
Troop transport ship (Custódio de Mello) (1957–2001)	G-22	MB *Soares Dutra*	9,464	127
Hydrographic vessel (Paraibano) (1968–1991)	H-11	MB *Paraibano*	32	11
Hydrographic vessel (Paraibano) (1968–1991)	H-12	MB *Rio Branco*	32	11
Hydrographic vessel (Paraibano) (1971–1991)	H-14	MB *Nogueira da Gama*	32	11
Hydrographic vessel (Paraibano) (1971–1991)	H-15	MB *Itacurussá*	32	11
Hydrographic vessel (Paraibano) (1972–1991)	H-16	MB *Camocim*	32	11
Hydrographic vessel (Paraibano) (1972–1991)	H-17	MB *Caravelas*	32	11
Beacon ship (Comandante Varella) (1982–present)	H-18	MB *Comandante Varella*	300	22
Beacon ship (Comandante Varella) (1983–present)	H-19	MB *Tenente Castelo*	300	22
Beacon ship (Comandante Varella) (1984–present)	H-20	MB *Comandante Manhães*	300	22
Hydrographic vessel (Sirius) (1958–present) (H)	H-21	MB *Sirius*	1,448	129
Hydrographic vessel (Sirius) (1958–1997) (H)	H-22	MB *Canopus*	1,463	102
Beacon ship (Santana) (1960–2001)	H-24	MB *Catelhanos*	110	7
Beacon ship (Comandante Varella) (1985–present)	H-25	MB *Tenente Boanerges*	300	22
Beacon ship (Santana) (1954–2001)	H-27	MB *Faroleiro Arêas*	110	7
Beacon ship (Santana) (1954–1977)	H-28	MB *Faroleiro Santana*	110	7

Beacon ship (Santana) (1954–1969)	H-29	MB *Faroleiro Wanderley*	110	7
Beacon ship (Santana) (1957–2001)	H-30	MB *Faroleiro Nascimento*	110	7
Hydrographic vessel (Argus) (1959–2004)	H-31	MB *Argus*	250	34
Hydrographic vessel (Argus) (1959–2001)	H-32	MB *Orión*	250	34
Hydrographic vessel (Argus) (1959–1996)	H-33	MB *Taurus*	250	34
Beacon ship (Santana) (1959–1963) (H)	H-34	MB *Faroleiro Getúlio Lima*	110	7
LCU (LCU 1610) (1978–1991)	L-10	MB *Guarapari*	190	14
LCU (LCU 1610) (1978–1991)	L-11	MB *Tambaú*	190	14
LCU (LCU 1610) (1981–1991)	L-12	MB *Camboriú*	190	14
LCU (LCU 1610) (1981–1991)	L-13	MB *Tramandaí*	190	14
LCVP Higgins boats (1955–1984)	P-501 to 534	-	8,200	4+36
(H) rear helicopter deck; (M) missiles				

TABLE 21: Brazilian Naval Aviation Aircraft Designations[10]	
Aircraft Type	***Aviação Naval Brasileira* designation**
Westland WS-S1/S2 Widgeon	HUW and later UH-1
Bell 47J	HUL-1 and later UH-3
Kawasaki-Bell 47G-3	HTL-6 and later IH-1
Grumman TBM-3E Avenger	-
Westland WS-55 Whirlwind Series 1	HU2W
Bell 47D-1	HTL-5
Taylorcraft BC-12D	-
CAP-4 Paulistinha	-
Fairchild PT-26	-
North American T-28R-1/T-28A Trojan	-
Pilatus P-3.04	-
Hughes 269A	HTH-1 and later IH-2
Hughes 269A-1	IH-2A
Hugues 269B	IH-2B
Sikorsky S-55C	HUS
Sikorsky SH-34J	SH-34J
Westland Wasp Series 3	SH-2, UH-2 & UH-2A
Westland WS-55 Whirlwind Series 3	SH-3 and later UH-5
Fairchild Hiller FH-1100	UH-4
Sikorsky S-61D-4 Sea King	SH-3A
Agusta-Sikorsky ASH-3D Sea King	SH-3B
Sikorsky SH-3D Sea King	SH-3B
Bell 206B Jet Ranger II	IH-6, IH-6A and later UH-6
Westland Sea Lynx HAS Mk.21	SAH-11
Westland Super Lynx Mk.21A	AH-11A
Helibrás HB350B/BA Esquilo	UH-12
UH= utility helicopter, IH= trainer helicopter, SH= ASW helicopter, AH= attack helicopter	

APPENDIX IV: Brazilian Military Ranks

TABLE 22: Brazilian Armed Forces Ranks (Officers)[11]

Brazilian Army	Brazilian Navy	Brazilian Air Force
Marechal (Marshal) (*)	*Almirante* (Admiral) (*)	*Marechal do Ar* (Air Marshal) (*)
General de Exército (General of the Army)	*Almirante de Esquadra* (Squadron Admiral)	*Tenente-Brigadeiro do Ar* (Air Lieutenant Brigadier)
General de Divisão (Major General)	*Vice-Almirante* (Vice Admiral)	*Major-Brigadeiro do Ar* (Air Major Brigadier)
General de Brigada (Brigadier General)	*Contra-Almirante* (Rear Admiral)	*Brigadeiro* (Brigadier)
Coronel (Colonel)	*Capitão de Mar e Guerra* (Captain of Sea and War)	*Coronel* (Colonel)
Tenente-Coronel (Lieutenant Colonel)	*Capitão de Fragata* (Frigate Captain)	*Tenente-Coronel* (Lieutenant Colonel)
Major (Major)	*Capitão de Corveta* (Corvette Captain)	*Major* (Major)
Capitão (Captain)	*Capitão-Tenente* (Captain-Lieutenant)	*Capitão* (Captain)
Primeiro Tenente (First Lieutenant)	*Primeiro Tenente* (First Lieutenant)	*Primeiro Tenente* (First Lieutenant)
Segundo Tenente (Second Lieutenant)	*Segundo Tenente* (Second Lieutenant)	*Segundo Tenente* (Second Lieutenant)
Aspirante a Oficial (Officer Candidate)	*Guarda-Marinha* (Midshipman)	*Aspirante a Oficial* (Officer Candidate)
(*) These highest ranks were given to the meritorious officers in case of war and other conflicts		

TABLE 23: Brazilian Armed Forces Ranks (NCOs and Other Ranks)[12]

Brazilian Army	Brazilian Navy	Brazilian Air Force
Subtenente (Sub Lieutenant)	*Sub-Oficial* (Chief NCO)	*Suboficial* (Chief NCO)
Primeiro Sargento (First Sergeant)	*Primeiro Sargento* (First Sergeant)	*Primeiro Sargento* (First Sergeant)
Segundo Sargento (Second Sergeant)	*Segundo Sargento* (Second Sergeant)	*Segundo Sargento* (Second Sergeant)
Terceiro Sargento (Third Sergeant)	*Terceiro Sargento* (Third Sergeant)	*Terceiro Sargento* (Third Sergeant)
Taifeiro-Mor (Service Chief)	*Cabo* (Corporal)	*Cabo* (Corporal)
Cabo (Corporal)	*Marinheiro* (Sailor)	*Taifeiro-Mor* (Service Chief)
Taifeiro de Primeira Classe (Service 1st Class)	-	*Soldado de Primeira Classe* (1st Class Soldier)
Taifeiro de Segunda Classe (Service 2nd Class)	-	*Taifeiro de Primeira Classe* (Service 1st Class)
Soldado (Soldier)	-	*Soldado de Segunda Classe* (2nd Class Soldier)
-	-	*Taifeiro de Segunda Classe* (Service 2nd Class)

TABLE 24: Brazilian Military Police Ranks[13]	
Officers	**NCOs/other ranks**
Comandante-Geral (General Commander)	*Primeiro Sargento* (First Sergeant)
Coronel (Colonel)	*Segundo Sargento* (Second Sergeant)
Tenente-Coronel (Lieutenant Colonel)	*Terceiro Sargento* (Third Sergeant)
Major (Major)	*Cabo* (Corporal)
Capitão (Captain)	*Soldado* (Soldier)
Primeiro Tenente (First Lieutenant)	-
Segundo Tenente (Second Lieutenant)	-
Aspirante a Oficial (Officer Candidate)	-
Subtenente (Sub Lieutenant)	-

TABLE 25: Brazilian Federal Police Ranks[14]	
Officers	**NCOs**
Diretor-Geral (General Director)	*Agente Classe Especial* (Special Class Agent)
Diretor (Director)	*Agente Primeira Classe* (First Class Agent)
Coordenador-Geráis (General Coordinator)	*Agente Segunda Clase* (Second Class Agent)
Coordenador (Coordinator)	*Agente Terceira Class* (Third Class Agent)
Chefe de Divisão (Division Chief)	-
Chefe de Serviço (Service Chief)	-
Chefe de Seção (Section Chief)	-
Chefe de Setor (Sector Chief)	-
Chefe de Núcleo (Nucleus Chief)	-

NOTES

Chapter 1

1 Thomas E. Skidmore, *The Politics of Military Rule in Brazil, 1964–1985* (New York: Oxford University Press, 1988).
2 Thomas E. Skidmore, *The Politics of Military Rule in Brazil, 1964–1985* (New York: Oxford University Press, 1988).
3 Elio Gaspari, *A Ditadura Envergonhada. As Ilusões Armadas*, Vol. I (São Paulo: Cia das Letras, 2002).
4 Herbert S. Klein & Francisco Vidal Luna: *Brazil 1964–1985. The Military Regimes of Latin American in the Cold War* (London: Yale University Press, 2017).
5 Herbert S. Klein & Francisco Vidal Luna: *Brazil 1964–1985.*
6 Herbert S. Klein & Francisco Vidal Luna: *Brazil 1964–1985.*
7 Herbert S. Klein & Francisco Vidal Luna: *Brazil 1964–1985.*
8 For fuller details of the Argentina's Triple A organisation see volumes 1 and 2 of the Latin America@War series *Operativo Independencia.*

Chapter 2

1 Elio Gaspari, *A Ditadura Envergonhada. As Ilusões Armadas*, Vol. I (São Paulo: Cia das Letras, 2002).

Chapter 3

1 https://www.eb.mil.br/republica
2 https://pt.wikipedia.org/wiki/Exercito_Brasileiro
3 https://tanks-encyclopedia.com/coldwar/brazilian-tanks/
4 https://www.armasnacionais.com.html
5 https://www.fab.mil.br/ex-comandantes
6 INCAER, *Historia Geral da Aeronáutica Brasileira*, Coleção Aeronáutica, Vol. 6 (Rio de Janeiro: Instituto Histórico-Cultural da Aeronáutica, 2022).
7 https://www.marinha.mil.br/
8 https://es.wikipedia.org/wiki/Marina_de_Brasil
9 Jackson Flores Jr, *Aeronaves Militares Brasileiras 1916–2015* (Rio de Janeiro: Action Editora, 2015).
10 Jackson Flores Jr, *Aeronaves Militares Brasileiras 1916–2015* (Rio de Janeiro: Action Editora, 2015).
11 https://pt.wikipedia.org/wiki/Policia_Federal_do_Brasil

Appendeces

1 https://pt.wikipedia.org/wiki/Reorganizao_do_Exercito_Brasileiro_na_ditadura_militar
2 https://pt.wikipedia.org/wiki/Reorganizao_do_Exercito_Brasileiro_na_ditadura_militar
3 https://pt.wikipedia.org/wiki/Reorganizao_do_Exercito_Brasileiro_na_ditadura_militar
4 https://pt.wikipedia.org/wiki/Reorganizao_do_Exercito_Brasileiro_na_ditadura_militar
5 https://pt.wikipedia.org/wiki/Reorganizao_do_Exercito_Brasileiro_na_ditadura_militar
6 https://pt.wikipedia.org/wiki/Reorganizao_do_Exercito_Brasileiro_na_ditadura_militar
7 Jackson Flores Jr, *Aeronaves Militares Brasileiras 1916–2015* (Rio de Janeiro: Action Editora, 2015).
8 Jackson Flores Jr, *Aeronaves Militares Brasileiras 1916–2015* (Rio de Janeiro: Action Editora. 2015).
9 https://www.naval.com.br/ngb/class.htm
10 Jackson Flores Jr, *Aeronaves Militares Brasileiras 1916–2015* (Rio de Janeiro: Action Editora. 2015).
11 https://www.eb.mil.br/postos-e-graduacoes
12 https://www.eb.mil.br/postos-e-graduacoes
13 https://www.sociedademilitar.com.br/
14 https://www.sociedademilitar.com.br/

SOURCES

Books

Amorin de Angelo, Vítor, *Luta Armada no Brasil*, Coleção Saber de Tudo (São Paulo: Editora Claridade, 2009)

Andrade, John M., *Latin-American Military Aviation*, 1st Edition (Leicester: Midland Counties Publications, 1982)

Butler, Phil & Dan Hagedorn, *Air Arsenal North America. Aircraft for the Allies 1938–1945. Purchases and Lend-Lease* (Hinckley, UK: Midland Publishing, 2004)

Cabral, Pedro Corrêa, *Xambioá – Guerrilha no Araguaia* (Rio de Janeiro: Editora Record, 1993)

Camazano Alamino, Cel. Av. (Ret.) Aparecido, *A Saga dos Guerreiros Polivalentes. Aviação de Reconhecimento e Ataque na FAB*, No. 38. (Rio de Janeiro: Instituto Histórico-Cultural da Aeronáutica/INCAER, 2015)

Camazano Alamino, Cel. Av. (Ret.) Aparecido, *Gloster Meteor. O Primero Jato do Brasil*, 1ª Edição (São Paulo: C&R Editorial, 2010)

Carvalho, Luiz Maklouf, *O Coronel Rompe o Silencio* (Rio de Janeiro: Editora Objetiva, 2004)

Castro, Celso, *A Invenção do Exército Brasileiro*, Serie Descubrindo o Brasil (São Paulo: Editora Zahar, 2002)

Corrêa Cabral, Captain (Ret.) Pedro, *Justicia e Democracia: as novas perspectivas da hermenêutica constitucional*, Vol. II (Raleigh, NC: Lulu Publishing, 2017)

Flores Jr, Jackson, *Aeronaves Militares Brasileiras 1916–2015* (Rio de Janeiro: Action Editora, 2015)

Flores Jr, Jackson, *Aviação Naval Brasileira* (Rio de Janeiro: Action Editora, 1995)

Gaspari, Elio, *A Ditadura Envergonhada. As Ilusões Armadas*, Vol. I (São Paulo: Cia das Letras, 2002)

Gaspari, Elio, *A Ditadura Escancarada. As Ilusões Armadas*, Vol. II (São Paulo: Cia das Letras, 2003)

Gaspari, Elio, *A Ditadura Derrotada. O Sacerdote e o Feiticeiro*, Vol. III (São Paulo: Cia das Letras, 2004)

Gaspari, Elio, *A Ditadura Encurralada. O Sacerdote e o Feiticeiro*, Vol. IV (São Paulo: Cia das Letras, 2002)

Gaspari, Elio, *A Ditadura Acabada*, Vol. V (São Paulo: Cia das Letras, 2016)

Hagedorn, Dan, *Texans and Harvards in Latin America* (West Sussex, UK: Air Britain Historians Ltd, 2009)

Hagedorn, Dan & Mario Overall, *Douglas DC-3/C-47 in Latin American Military Service* (Manchester: Crécy Publishing Ltd, 2021)

Higuchi, Hélio, Reginaldo Bacchi & Paulo Roberto Bastos Jr., *O Stuart No Brasil. M3/M3A1 e derivados*, 1ª Edição (São Paulo: Tecnodefesa Editorial Ltda, 2015)

Higuchi, Hélio & Paulo Roberto Bastos Jr., *M4 Sherman No Brasil*, Grandes Armas (São Paulo: C&R Editorial, 2008)

INCAER, *Historia Geral da Aeronáutica Brasileira*, Coleção Aeronáutica, Vol. 5 (Rio de Janeiro: Instituto Histórico-Cultural da Aeronáutica, 2014)

INCAER, *Historia Geral da Aeronáutica Brasileira*, Coleção Aeronáutica, Vol. 6 (Rio de Janeiro: Instituto Histórico-Cultural da Aeronáutica, 2022)

Klein, Herbert S. & Francisco Vidal Luna, *Brazil 1964–1985. The Military Regimes of Latin American in the Cold War* (London: Yale University Press, 2017)

Lavenére-Wanderley, Tenente-Brigadeiro R/R Nelson Freire, *História da Força Aérea Brasileira*, 2a. Edição (Rio de Janeiro: INCAER, 1975)

Lorch, Carlos, *Fuzileiros Navais, Brazil's Amphibious Warriors* (Rio de Janeiro: Action Editora, 1999)

Mattos de Abreu, Guilherme; Barbosa Junior, Ilques; de Senna Bittencourt, Armando; Carmo Cesar, William; Gomes dos Santos Filho, Pedro; Eduardo Alves de Almeida, Francisco; de Sousa Moreira, William; Laura Costa Nogueira da Gama, Edina; Oliveira Castro, Alceu; Jungstedt; Paulo da Cunha Castro, Pierre; André Lopes da Silva, Carlos; dos Santos Guimarães, Ricardo; José Gomes Loureiro, Marcello; Homero Fonseca de Castro, Adler; & de Freitas e Gonzaga da Silva, Jéssica, *Marinha do Brasil: Uma Síntese Histórica* (Rio de Janeiro: Serviço de Documentação da Marinha, 2022)

Monteiro, Adalberto *et al.*, *Guerrilha do Araguaia* (São Paulo: Anita Garibaldi Editora, 2005)

Morais, Taís & Eumano Silva, *Operação Araguaia. Os Arquivos Secretos da Guerrilha* (São Paulo: Geração Editorial, 2011)

Nascimento, Durbens, *A Guerrilha do Araguaia 1967–1975. Paulistas e Militares na Amazonía* (Belém, Pará: NAEA Editora, 2021)

Nascimento, José & Licio Maciel, *Orvil Tentativas De Tomada Do Poder* (Salto, SP: Editora Schoba, 2009)

Pereira Netto, Francisco C., *Aviação Militar Brasileira 1916–1984* (Rio de Janeiro: Revista Aeronáutica Editora, 1984)

Portela, Fernando, *Guerras e Guerrilhas no Brasil* (São Paulo: Global Editora, 1979)

Skidmore, Thomas E., *The Politics of Military Rule in Brazil, 1964–1985* (New York: Oxford University Press, 1988)

Studart, Hugo, *A lei da selva: estratégias, imaginário e discurso dos militares sobre a guerrilha do Araguaia* (São Paulo: Geração Editorial, 2006)

Ustra, Carlos Alberto Brilhante, *A Verdade Sufocada* (Brasília: Editora Ser, 2006)

Articles

De Almeida Teles, Janaina, 'Secrets and Myths about the Araguaia Guerrilla War' (1972–1974), *Historia Unisinos*, Vol. 18, No. 3 (Universidade do Vale do Rio dos Sinos, São Leopoldo, September-December 2014)

De Souza Pinheiro, Cel. EB Álvaro, 'Guerrilla in the Brazilian Amazon', *FMSO Publications* (Foreign Military Studies Office, Fort Leavenworth, KS, July 1995)

Maklouf Carvalho, Cel. FAB Luiz, 'A FAB usou Napalm no Araguaia', *Air & Space Power Journal* (1998)

Munhoz Svartman, Eduardo, 'Brazil–United States Relations during the Cold War: Political Dynamic and Arms Transfers', *Brazilian Political Science Review (BPSR)*, Vol. 5, No.2 (2011, Associação Brasileira de Ciencia Política, São Paulo)

Navarro V, Lic. Agustín, 'Los Grupos Revolucionarios del Brasil', *Temas Contemporáneos*, Año XVI, No. 198 (México: Instituto de Investigaciones Sociales y Económicas A.C., 1971)

Pinheiro, Coronel Álvaro de Souza, *Guerrilha na Amazônia: Uma Experiência no Passado, Presente e o Futuro* (Washington, DC: Air Power Journal, edição trimestral de abril/maio/junho, 1995)

Teló, Fabricio, 'Campesinos, emociones y tentativas de resistencia armada a la dictadura empresarial-militar de Brasil', *Polis*

Revista Latinoamericana, No. 53, Centro de Investigación Sociedad y Políticas Públicas (CISPO) (31 May 2019, Universidad Federal Rural de Rio de Janeiro)

Conferences

Morales, Vanessa, 'Las Guerrillas de Araguaia. La última guerrilla comunista'. Conference during the XIII Jornadas de Sociología, Facultad de Ciencias Sociales, Universidad de Buenos Aires, Buenos Aires, 2019

Nercesian, Inés, 'Nueva Izquierda en Brasil en los años 60'. Conference during the VI Jornadas de Sociología, Facultad de Ciencias Sociales, Universidad de Buenos Aires, Buenos Aires, 2004

University Papers

Almeida, Thamyris F.T., *Araguaia: Maoist Uprising and Military Counterinsurgency in the Brazilian Amazon, 1967–1975* (Master's Degree thesis, University of Massachusetts Amherst, July 2015)

Oliveira, Juliano, *Força Aérea Brasileira: doctrina e estrutura da geopolítica do Prata a Amazónia, 1964–2003)* (Master's Degree thesis, Universidade Estadual Paulista/UNESP, Franca, SP, 2005)

Pessoa Campos Filho, Romualdo, *A Esquerda em Armas: História da Guerrilha do Araguaia (1972–1975)*, Dissertação apresentada no curso de pós-graduação do Instituto de Ciências Humanas e Letras da Universidade Federal de Goiás para o mestrado em História das Sociedades Agrárias em fevereiro de 1995

Web Pages

Araguaia Guerrilla, at https://www.todamateria.com.br/guerrilha-do-araguaia/

Brazilian Army reorganization, at https://pt.wikipedia.org/wiki/Reorganizao_do_Exercito_Brasileiro_na_ditadura_militar

Brazilian tanks and armored vehicles, at https://tanks-encyclopedia.com/coldwar/brazilian-tanks/

Brazilian Naval Aviation, at
https://asassobreosmares.rudnei.cunha.nom.br/category/historia/

https://www.jornalopcao.com.br/colunas-e-blogs/imprensa/ordem-pra-matar-na-guerrilha-do-araguaia-era-do-presidente-emilio-medici-diz-o-coronel-pedro-cabral-426274/

'Guerrilha na Amazonía: Uma experiencia no pasado, o presente e o fututo', article published by Cel. Álvaro de Souza Pinheiro do Exército Brasileiro in November 2005 at https://www.defesanet.com.br/geopolitica/noticia/5193/toa-guerrilha-na-amazonia-a-experiencia-dos-anos-70-parte-2/

Brazilian Navy ships, at
https://pt.wikipedia.org/wiki/Lista_de_navios_descomissionados_da_Marinha_do_Brasil

Brazilian police forces, at
https://pt.wikipedia.org/wiki/Forças_policiais_do_Brasil

ABOUT THE AUTHOR

Antonio Luis Sapienza Fracchia was born in Asunción, Paraguay, on 14 May 1960. He graduated from the Catholic University of Asunción, where he got a B.A. in Clinical Psychology. He also took specialised English courses at Tulane University in New Orleans, Louisiana, and teaching methodology courses at San Diego State University in California. He is now retired but worked for nearly 40 years as an English teacher and one of the academic coordinators at the *Centro Cultural Paraguayo-Americano* (CCPA), a binational institute in Asunción. Married with two children, he resides in the capital. He is an aviation historian who has written more than 500 articles in specialised magazines and web pages on the history of Paraguayan aviation and has given numerous lectures in schools, universities, institutes and military and civil institutions in Paraguay and abroad. Since 2004, he has been an aviation history professor in the Paraguayan Air Force (FAP). In August 2023, he was appointed Corresponding Academician of the Paraguayan Academy of History. He has published 27 books since 1996, this being his 14th with Helion. He has received a total of seven decorations for his academic merits: two from Argentina, one from Brazil and four from his own country, Paraguay (two from the Air Force, one from the Naval Aviation and one from the Civil Aviation Authority DINAC).